Normandy
lace patchworks

Revised Edition

THE LACE MERCHANT
THE ULTIMATE STUDY GUIDES
for those who enjoy old lace

**This book is dedicated
to the connoisseurs of vintage lace:**

*To those who love unraveling the mysteries of these beautiful crafts, and
especially to those who made this book possible by sharing their lace,
information, photographs, and leads for more research.*

Acknowledgements

Jeri Ames, Connie Brown, Judy Cody, Catherine Daniels,
Jane Dilks, Olivene Hargrave, Mary Ann Layne, Joann
Leonard, Denise Liberio, Devon M. Thein, Nancy Thurmon,
Anne Richards, Susanna Urlik

Colonial Coverlet Guild of America

Despina Forou-Koutsika, author of *Lace in Chios*,
published in 2000 by Friends of the Villages of Chios.

ISBN 978-0-9642871-7-4
*Connoisseur's Guide to
Normandy Lace Patchworks*
Revised Edition
Copyright 2005 Elizabeth M. Kurella

Editor: Rose Anne Warner

Published by
The Lace Merchant
P.O. Box 224
Whiting, IN 46394

www.lacemerchant.com

When we hoard and hide our best treasures
They grow tender and fragile apace.
Tis the giving, the using, the blending
that assign them a glorified place.

Ruth de Young, Chicago Tribune, 1933

The need to share their treasured but frayed old collars, handkerchiefs, cuffs, doilies, and just scraps – to bring them out of storage and into daylight where their craftmanship and beauty could be enjoyed and the memories wrapped in their stitches could be kept alive – prompted women in the early 20th century to stitch those bits into lace patchworks.

One of the most glorious of fabrics ever to grace a patchwork is the French *fond du bonet*. This translucent muslin, heavily embroidered and accented with needle lace, was used in caps and bonnets in 19th century Normandy, and recycled in patchworks after it became frayed or out of fashion.

Although the terms *Normandy Lace* and *Normandy Work* rarely appeared in print, they persist as a popular, word-of-mouth descriptive term for lace patchworks. Thus the choice of name for this book.

Contents

Introduction	7
Retrospective	8
Classic French	10
Commercial European	12
American Artisanal	14
Commemorative	19
Greek Lace Mosaics	22
Looking at Lace Patchworks	24
Structure	26
Ways of Planning Lace Patchworks	28
Materials	32
Judging Intrinsic Worth	40
Materials	42
Design	44
Technique and Workmanship	48
Condition	50
Rarity and Market Value	53
Gallery	54
Simple Gifts	56
Unfinished Symphony	60
Texas Treasures	62
Mary Martin's Mother's Tablecloth	64
Bows and Buttons	66
Rose Anne's Round	69
Second Hand Rose	72
Forever and a Day	74

Emily's Missing Masterpieces	76
Jane's Gift	78
Whitework Wonderland	80
Quartet	84
Collector's Quarry	86
Connoisseur's Choice	90
Mother's Prize	96
After the War Was Over	100
Vive le Difference	104
Le Baseball Diamond	107
Floral Fireworks	110
Ouiseaux Extraordinaire	114
Faux French	118
Grace	122
Grecian Ladies	124
Living with Lace Patchworks	126
Washing Lace Patchworks	128
Mending Lace Patchworks	130
Making Lace Patchworks Today	146
Preparing the Lace	148
Preparing to Play	149
Step by Step	150
Index	154

Introduction

When I presented an exhibit of Normandy Lace pillow shams, doilies, and lamp shades that I had designed and made I was astonished to find that many people could not see them as patchworks of lace the way they see quilts as patchworks of fabrics. The substance called "lace" is an optical illusion, and sometimes a very peculiar substance to comprehend.

Get a firm grip on the following sequence of events. It will make it much easier to understand that peculiar substance of lace in general, and Normandy lace patchworks in particular.

■ Thread manipulations are combined to make bits and pieces of lace.

■ Bits and pieces of lace are combined to make lace things.

■ Lace things are recycled to make patchworks.

Thread manipulations, bits and pieces of lace, lace things, patchworks.

The thread manipulations are stitching, weaving, twisting and knotting traveling under the names of needle lace, bobbin lace, filet, and crochet, tatting and other techniques of lacemaking.

Collars, tablecloths, fan leaves -- any kind of lace thing might be assembled from a combination of several of these manipulations. Crochet and tatting were often combined in little doilies. Bobbin lace leaves might be combined with needle lace roses and the whole thing embedded in a needle lace mesh background and made into a veil. Little machine-made strips of lace often were shaped into flowers and pinwheels with crochet or needle lace stitches and then made into collars and cuffs or doilies.

That intermediate step – bits and pieces of lace combined to make lace things – is what makes the whole process so dazzling. The shredding lace collar being cut up to join with lengths of lace yardage and cut bits of a lace dresser scarf already might have been a combination of different kinds of laces. A patchwork being recycled into another patchwork.

So it is not so surprising that magic happens when old lace is recycled. The patchwork of patchworks becomes a new kind of lace which we call Normandy Lace. Learn to see beyond the optical illusion, and a marvelous new universe will open to you.

Retrospective

Retrospective – why such a pretentious word instead of simply *history*? History implies a very specific presentation of dates, events, places. The information on lace patchworks is not definitive enough to offer that. There is remarkably little published information on lace patchworks; especially any that specifically use the terms *Normandy Lace* or *Normandy Work*.

Using the word "patchwork" rather than "piecework" in this book was another deliberate choice. One distinguishing feature of the lace compositions called Normandy Lace is that they are assembled mostly from bits and scraps with cut edges, rather than from shaped whole insertions with finished edges.

For centuries, large lace tablecloths, altar cloths and bed hangings were assembled from many smaller pieces of lace. Triangles, squares, rectangles of lace were made and inserted into fabric, or sewn together directly.

The tablecloth shown at the top of the opposite page is assembled from pieces of lace which are separate and complete. Different techniques of lacemaking were used make them. Take apart the top tablecloth and it will yield individual triangles, squares, rectangles and strips of different laces. Take apart the tablecloth at the bottom, and it will yield cut bits and scraps.

In the nineteenth century the western world was awash in damaged and out-of-fashion old lace. Appreciation for the handwork was shown by continuing to keep it visible and useful. Good bits of lace from frayed yardage, collars, handkerchiefs and other items were cut up and recycled.

Documentation has not surfaced to tell us who made most of these patchworks, and when and where. By looking at clues in the designs and materials, techniques and workmanship in the old pieces we can make some guesses.

Patchwork vs. Piecework: Tablecloth at the bottom is assembled from bits, scraps, and patches. Tablecloth at the top is made from individual finished pieces designed to fit the overall plan.

■ **Classic French**
Includes *fond du bonet* that was antique at the time the patchwork was made.

■ **American Artisanal**
Includes a wide assortment of designs and materials.

■ **Commercial European**
Made from all new material; design might be template based or opportunistic.

■ **Greek Lace Mosaics**
Typically include many craft laces.

■ **Commemorative Lace Patchworks**
Feature symbols, crests, and monograms that identify the group and its members; includes a wide variety of materials.

Classic French

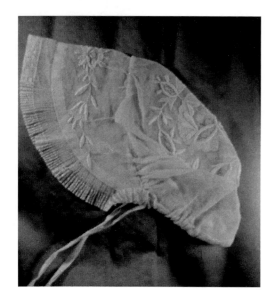

The centerpiece and focus points in some of the most beautiful lace patchworks are the round embroidered lace-like backs of French caps from Brittany and Normandy known as *fond du bonet*.

These confections of lacy embroidery – fine white muslin far too heavily embroidered for their own good and accented with amazing insertions of hand stitched needle lace – were pieced together with yards and yards of vintage Valenciennes, Mechlin, and Bucks Point edgings and other old laces, both handmade and machine. Other times, the connecting links were new yardage.

Nineteenth century caps of Normandy and Britanny yielded distinctive plate-sized rounds of fond du bonet *from the backs, and and half-moons from the top front. Whitework embroidery was recycled into classic French patchworks in the early twentieth century.*

Rounds of heavy embroiderry with lace insertions – this one has inserts of bobbin and machine made lace – are characteristic of original fond du bonet.

Bedspreads, pillow shams, tablecloths, runners, lamp shades, doilies: anything imaginable was being produced in these magical patchworks. Because they contained original French *fond du bonet* and were one-of-a kind it suggests individual artisanal work, or a very small industry, likely in France. But where and exactly when?

Unconfirmed stories abound that these patchworks were sold to U.S. doughboys at the end of World War I to bring home as souvenirs. Common sense says a lot of it probably was and did. What would be more logical than war-torn and impoverished French digging into their family treasures for things to sell to the relatively wealthy U.S. soldiers? With luck, documented stories will emerge

Whatever the arrangement of the patches, the key characteristic of classic French Normandy Lace was the presence of dinner-plate sized rounds that likely are recycled backs of 19th century Breton or Norman caps. Showy whitework embroideries were worked on fine muslin or on net. Heavy embroideries sometimes were rescued from shredded muslin and regrounded on fine cotton machine made net.

See page 40 for an overview of the bedspread this section is a part of.

Commercial European

At some unknown point in the early 1900s, the market demand for dazzling patchworks of lace seems to have outstripped the supply of old frayed French caps and bonnets.

A large percentage of the vintage lace patchworks found today are made from remarkably similar materials that appear to have been all new at the time they were made. An industry sprouted to embroider – by hand and by machine – muslin rounds, half-moons, and strips imitating the French *fond du bonet* sections. Miles of fine cotton lace insertion yardage and acres of frothy,

Above: Detail of tablecloth shown on opposite page. Edgings and insertions in the same pattern in different widths are a good clue that the patchwork was commercially produced. The background materials in this patchwork also are very typical of commercial patchworks.

Below: When all the whitework rounds have exactly the same relatively simple design, it is a good sign that the piece was commercially produced.

Retrospective

supple cotton embroidered net must have poured from factories directly into the patchwork market.

Similar designs of interconnected and complex geometric patterns appear over and over in these commercial patchworks, all worked in a handful of recognizable materials. This makes these patchworks relatively easy to place in time.

Because the materials were all new at the time the patchwork was assembled, many of these lovely lace pillow shams, bedspreads, tablecloths, table runners, and doilies are still usable today.

High-end department stores like Marshall Field in Chicago, Nieman Marcus in Texas, Wannamakers in Philadelphia, and B. Altman in New York all maintained boutique industries in Europe. A search of their pre-World War II archives likely would uncover their sources for these patchworks.

Early twentieth century lace patchworks like the one above were commercially produced in Europe, and sold in fine department stores in the United States. The design is a popular geometric template defined with edgings and insertions like those shown on the opposite page and on page 39. Embroidered muslin and net designs are relatively simple. For a comparison of simple commercial whiteworks and original fond du bonet *see the Materials section starting on page 32.*

13

American Artisanal

The fad of lace patchwork-making traveled from France to the United States in the early 1900s. A rage for do-it-yourself lace patchworks clearly was inspired by the original patchworks of French whitework *fond du bonet*, but they no longer included any of the whitework. The patchwork-makers were not hampered by this lack of round lacy embroideries. They simply used what lace was at hand and contrived their own styles of patchworks. These American patchworks truly are a form of folk art, made without benefit of classes, pattern books, or instructions.

Articles on how to use bits and pieces of old lace to make new fashions occasionally appeared in magazines around the turn of the century. Sara Hadley, probably best known as the inventor of Royal Battenberg lace, wrote an article for the November 1908 issue of *Ladies Home Journal* presenting projects for using those bits and tatters of old lace that the owners simply could not bear to throw away. Hadley does not attribute the craft to lacemakers of Normandy or Brittany, but simply offers suggestions for *"Using Up Pieces of Old Lace."*

Hadley's instructions for making these patchworks seem remarkably terse today: "... the design has first been worked out in a conventional pattern by the inserts of fine beading on the sheerest of linen... Then follows the selection of your laces as to size and design and to fill in the spaces... "

Other instructions relate to thoughtfully arranging designs and grouping roses and other pattern bits of lace until "...gradually the laces will adapt themselves easily into symmetrical patterns, at the will of the worker, until the finished pieces become a triumph of art." Nothing is said of the actual stitching process.

Molly Millard, in a December, 1927 article in *Comfort* magazine, does attribute the craft and style of lace patchworks to the lacemakers of Normandy and Brittany. She calls the patchworks "Brittany Lace."

Without question, Millard must have read Hadley's 1908 article. Occasional phrases straight out of Hadley appear in Millard's instructions: "..Pin the different pieces in place and study the effect. Several changes in plans may be necessary before one gets just the right combinations, but by experimenting, gradually the laces will adapt themselves into a symmetrical pattern, at the will of the worker, until the finished pieces becomes a triumph of dainty beauty."

Her sewing instructions are just as terse: "When a design is fully planned for, baste all the different parts carefully to the foundation, and machine-stitch along either edge of the insertion bands." This last suggestion is curious. An artisanal machine-stitched lace patchwork has yet to surface.

In addition to reflecting materials already presented by Hadley decades earlier, Millard seems to be following rather than leading the patchwork makers. An unfinished patchwork found in a Texas antique

Retrospective

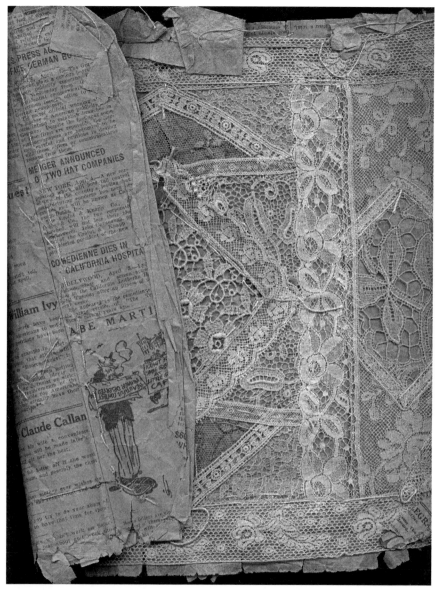

Work-in progress was backed with layers of newspaper to give it more stability. Crumbling newspaper, dated April 3, 1927, includes articles by Will Rogers and Edgar A. Guest. Dated months before Millard's article in Comfort *magazine (see following pages), it suggests she reflected rather than led the patchwork-makers.*

Retrospective

market is backed with a newspaper dated nearly a year before Millard's article appeared. Pieces like that work-in-progress are not uncommon in Texas. In the late 1920s, a group or perhaps groups of ladies in the Dallas-Fort Worth area of Texas were busy making lace patchworks.

A unique artisanal patchwork offered on ebay lead to information about Blanche Phillippi Cavender who was making lace patchworks in that area in the early 1900s. She is known to have made at least four lace patchwork tablecloths as wedding gifts for her children.

Another lace patchwork maker was profiled in an article in the *Oakland (California) Tribune* in the 1980s. Emily Teagle, a Texan transplanted in California began making patchworks in the 1920s. Her age is not given in the article, but judging from the photo taken in the 1980s, she must have been quite young when she was making the patchworks.

In this 1908 article in Ladies Home Journal, Sara Hadley offered suggestions for "Using Up Old Pieces of Lace." Hadley's projects included laces embedded in fabric in the style of French heirloom sewing, and patchworks made completely of lace pieces.

Retrospective

No information is available to know if the two were acquainted. The mother of actress Mary Martin also was making patchworks at that time in that general area. (Their patchworks are shown in the Gallery.)

These lace patchworks almost never include either real French cap backs or the commercial imitations. They include a great variety of lace pieces of all styles and technique. The overall design sometimes is a variation of a crazy quilt, but many times it is a thoughtful arrangement based on specific shaped insertions, medallions, and doilies used as focal points, and surrounded by bits and scraps.

Molly Millard, in a 1927 article in Comfort magazine, credits the lacemakers in the French regions of Normandy and Brittany with "solving the problem of utilizing such leftovers, in a way which is both practical and lovely."

Retrospective

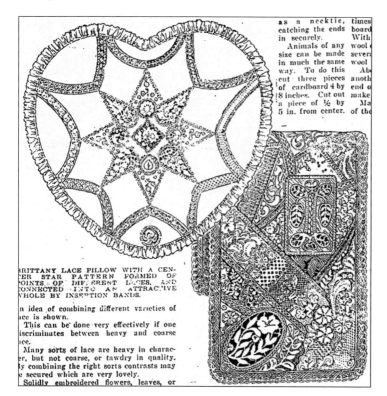

Patterns for lace pieceworks shown at left are from Molly Millard's December, 1927 article in Comfort *magazine.*

The pieced star in the center of Millard's heart shaped pillow is almost identical to the star in Sara Hadley's November, 1908 Ladies Home Journal article. The corner of Millard's crazy piecework pattern is almost identical to Hadley's piecework square, both shown below.

Commemorative

Large projects, especially tablecloths, were popular as group projects for women's clubs and other organizations. How many of these were made is fun to speculate about. Two examples exist just in the Chicago, Illnois area. Similar in their origins, andyet very different in style, each tablecloth reflects the spirit and style of the groups that made them.

The Colonial Coverlet Guild of America (CCGA) is dedicated to the study and preservation of the homespun, linsey-woolsey style of 19th century coverlets. In the 1930s gifts of lace bits were solicited from members, and hundreds and hundreds were received, including lace collars, doilies, edging, insertions, cuffs, vestees, medallions, and fragments. An article that appeared in the CCGA's newsletter so beautifully captured the spirit of this project – why and how it was made – that it is reprinted on the following pages along with pictures of the tablecloth. The article appeared in the February 1996 newsletter at a time the tablecloth was exhibited at one of their guild meetings. The tablecloth is now in the DuPage County Museum in Wheaton, Illinois.

A 1933 *Chicago Tribune* article describes a similar project, a twelve-foot tablecloth completed by the Chicago Woman's Club, containing lace mementos donated by members of the club. The verse quoted on the cover of this book: "the giving, the using the blending" of treasured old lace bits begins the Tribune article by Ruth de Young that describes the project. "... Mrs.

Shirk, whose interest in lace and fine needlework is well known, suggested to the house committee that an exquisite cloth could be made out of the scraps of lace laid away in family vaults and dresser drawers."

"Gifts of lace for the cloth," de Young continues, "were donated by 178 persons, many of the members of Chicago's pioneer families. There are headdress and collars, fragments of lace fans and waists, nightcaps, and handkerchiefs sewn into the delicate whole." Nineteenth century Duchesse, Rosaline, Honiton, Point de Gaze, and other high-fashion lace handkerchiefs, lappets, collars and cuffs are embedded in the tablecloth. Most extraordinary are the dozen plus of doilies of handmade bobbin and needle lace bearing the initials of prominent member's families. A separate little piece bears the initials CWC for the Chicago Woman's Club.

When that group disbanded in the late 1990s, the tablecloth was given to the Chicago Historical Society along with their archives, and now is part of their permanent collection.

The emphasis in this project, as it seems to be with many of these patchworks, is on the symbolism of working together in compansionship; saving and sharing treasured memories; and respecting and showing off beautiful handwork. They also are an enduring testimonial to the importance of the tea social as the women's answer to the power lunch of the mid to late twentieth century.

An Explanation of the Reason For and the History of This Collection of Laces

Reprinted with permission from the February, 1996 issue of the newsletter of the Colonial Coverlet Guild of America.

In the Colonial Coverlet Guild of America's year book for the year 1931-32 appears the following: A delightful idea for our guild comes from our member, Mrs. Charles Bohasseck. All members are invited to participate. Through the years we have lacked an official cloth for our friendly dish of tea, and Mrs. Bohasseck will design for us a tea cloth composed of pieces of lace and embroidered edging, insertions or medallions, sent in by our members. No piece is too small, nor too large for acceptance. The only restriction is silk lace which, because of it's texture, would not give the wear of flax or cotton. A chart will be made to keep forever and a day, as a guild record, with the name of each contributor placed in that section of the design which is equivalent to the use of the donator's lace or embroidery. Kindly sew a piece of cotton on your gift containing your name, address and any interesting history you may care to give.

The ladies of the guild cooperated beautifully. The laces began to come in. So many were being received that the mailman, who delivered them, wondered what was going on. Much of the lace came without identification from the donors.

Mrs. B. opened these many different types of packages and envelopes and found laces in many shapes and conditions. Much of it was very soiled, some yellowed with age, some had been laundered and some had not been used. She sorted these laces, washed them and bleached them by putting them in mason jars filled with sudsy water and stood the jars in her sunporch windows and each time she went by a bottle she would shake it and set it back to bleach some more. When the material was clean and bleached to suit her she would take it out, rinse it thoroughly and then press it on a dry Turkish towel to take out the

Colonial Coverlet Guild trademark, worked by Edna Wilson Whitcomb in darning on cotton net. Dates on the tablecloth represent the organization's first ten years of existence.

excess water. She would then lay it on another dry towel and press and stretch it out with her hands until it was stretched right. She then went ahead to design the tea cloth, and this ambitious lady manipulated lace collars, doilies, edgings, insertions, cuffs, vestees, medallions etc. into a beautiful scalloped banquet-cloth.

Edna Wilson Whitcomb worked the Guild trademark in darning on cotton net. Mrs. A. M Davidson crocheted a filet insertion with the guild name. Mrs. A. Artkamper worked two squares of netting with the guild symbols. These three projects are integral parts of the now Banquet-cloth.

Many or most of the members of the Guild had a part in sewing the pieces of lace where Mrs. Bohassek indicated they should go, and many times at these meetings, where the sewing progressed, that "friendly dish of tea" was served on the completed part while the industrious ladies worked on sewing the lace.

In the 1950-51 yearbook: It represents twelve years of arduous labor – the collection of laces housed in four books are the pieces which could not be used in the cloth; these books consist of 73 pages of laces – 732 pieces, 499 patterns or designs.

The lace is of many kinds, some made with sewing needles, pillow and bobbin, tatting shuttle, crochet hook, knitting needle, netting needle. punch and needle. A few are machine made. They go by the names of Torchon, Teneriffe, Armenian, Venetian, Spanish, Tatting, Netting, Cretan or fagoting. Bobbin or pillow lace, French Valenciennes, needle lace, embroidery on net, crocheting, Maltese lace, Drawnwork, cutwork, filet, Battenberg, Schiffle embroidery, Swiss embroidery and hand embroidery. One can imagine that many stories and much history lies in back of many of these pieces. At least this collection is a real reminder of the result of cooperation and willing work of a group banded together for companionship, information and good work. Would that there were many more organizations like the Colonial Coverlet Guild of America.

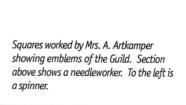

Squares worked by Mrs. A. Artkamper showing emblems of the Guild. Section above shows a needleworker. To the left is a spinner.

Greek Lace Mosaics

Laces of all kinds – needle lace, bobbin lace, bebilla knotted lace, filet darned networks, crochet – have been made for decades on the Greek island of Chios in the eastern Aegean sea. It should be no surprise that an island with magnificent mosaics of colorful glass bits on their ancient monastery walls should follow that art form to use bits and pieces of all these handmade lace to make patchworks, or "lace mosaics." This tradition has continued to the present day, and is detailed in a beautiful four-color book, *Lace in Chios*, by Despina Forou-Koutsika, published in 2000.

The Greek lace mosaics have a flavor distinctly different from the Western European and American patchworks. The wide variety of locally made laces dominate the mosaics. The simple, bold patterns of laces like filet, bebilla, torchon bobbin lace, needle lace, and crochet give an exhuberance and sharpness to the mosaics that is eyecatching and seems especially to invite touching.

To make the mosaics, pieces of lace were selected by thickness and pattern. Each piece was custom dyed with locally available vegetable dyes or tea to match others used in the same patchwork. The lace pieces were assembled into the desired patterns with small pieces of lace made specially to fill

Lace mosaic in the collection of Mrs. H. Stakias. Made in Chios in 1995 by Mrs. Moraitakis and Mrs. K. Stefanou.

gaps in the overall design. Lace bits were joined using a unique technique of short bars or "rice grains"

Each mosaic reflects the philosophy of the designer. Of mosaic-maker Eri Melekou, Koutsika relates "(she) always said that the lace for mosaic work should be left whole and should be made into larger articles. In this way, round, oval, and rectangular pieces were made. She also believed that each piece should be separated from the other by short joining bars so that the beauty of each piece could be seen."

A high point of the small commercial lace mosaic workshops seems to have been the 1930s through the 1950s. One of the best known designers was Eleni Kouvela, who organized exhibits in Athens and took orders for pieces to be made in workshops in Chios. Between 20 and 30 girls, taught the sewing techniques by Kouvela, were employed at that time.

Even today, a few lacemakers still make custom designed patchworks if the customer provides the vintage lace. Vintage pieces occasionally surface for sale on the island of Chios. The Monastery of Saint Constantinos, in the town of Karfa on Chios where some of the original vintage lace mosaics were made, occasionally offers a few pieces for sale.

Lace mosaic tablecloth from the book Lace in Chios *by Despina Forou-Koutsika. Reprinted with permission of the author.*

Looking at Lace Patchworks

Where do I put my eyes? That's the usual first question anyone has when faced with a complex lace patchwork. They are optical illusions, designed to dazzle, and it is helpful to have a plan for looking at them.

Train your eye to see the overall framework of the patchwork – the lines between the patches. Study the relationship between the pattern formed by the shapes of the patches and the lines that frame them, and by the patterns in the lace pieces and strips of lace themselves.

Design in lace patchworks differs from fabric patchworks in several respects. In lace patchworks, the overall framework or skeleton-like lines of the patchwork are interrelated with the patterns in the lace pieces in a way that almost never happens in a calico patchwork.

Try to determine by looking at the overall plan and the lace pieces that make it up which came first in designing and making the patchwork: the unique lace pieces with their particular shape, design or pattern and texture, or the overall plan.

In the first case, which I call an "opportunistic" patchwork, the maker arranged specific pieces of lace, perhaps collars, cuffs, fan leaf, a handkerchief corner, several doilies, on a large paper, then filled in the blanks between those specific pieces. In the second case, which I call a "template based" patchwork, the maker started with a template or pattern. Edgings and insertions form the lines of that template. Spaces are filled in with other laces, often bought specifically for that design.

Opportunistic patchworks more often were made by individuals as pieces of folk art. Template-based patchworks often were commercial, made to sell.

In a well-designed lace patchwork, the patterns within the lace pieces should enhance the overall design. There should be focus, background, and something that connects them.

Opposite page: Antimacassar tinted a deep rusty brown. Piece is very typical of American artisanal lace patchworks made in the late 1920s.

■ **Structure**
   Focus
   Framework or skeleton
   Background

■ **Ways of Planning Lace Patchworks**
   Template based
   Opportunistic

■ **Materials**
   Real *fond du bonet*
   Commercial imitation *fond du bonet*
   Handmade or machine?
   Vintage or comtemporary?

Structure

Focus

The centerpiece and focus of many lace patchworks is the *fond du bonet*, or French whitework. Other patchworks, especially artisanal ones, may be based around a unique lace doily, fan leaf, or other special lace piece.

Each patchwork may have several focal points; usually one centerpiece, and others in corners and sides. Judge the focus pieces on their own intrinsic worth and beauty, and on how they fit into the piecework.

Background

Most patchworks will have some areas of simple "fill in the blanks" or spaces between the important focus elements. For the design be most effective, these must contrast with the focus pieces and connecting insertions.

The background lace can have a very strong pattern or texture, as long as it doesn't dominate the overall design. Reverse designs, where the background is the focus, separated only by the insertion yardage, can be effective.

Framework or template

Template-based pieceworks are built around a skeleton of lace insertions and edgings. An edging typically surrounds the central focus piece, and defines the intersecting, overlapping geometric patterns.

The design of the framework should be interesting, with overlaps and links with all parts of the patchwork.

Even crazy patchworks and artisanal designs built up from doilies and fragments will use edgings and insertion lengths to join pieces, smooth out the rough edges, and provide some semblance of unity and order.

There should be enough contrast in the lace designs for the overall plan to emerge. If the background pattern is dense and busy, the framework lace should be simple and open. Dense, busy patterns in both the background and the framework obscure the overall plan.

Looking at Lace Patchworks

Focus

Framework

Background

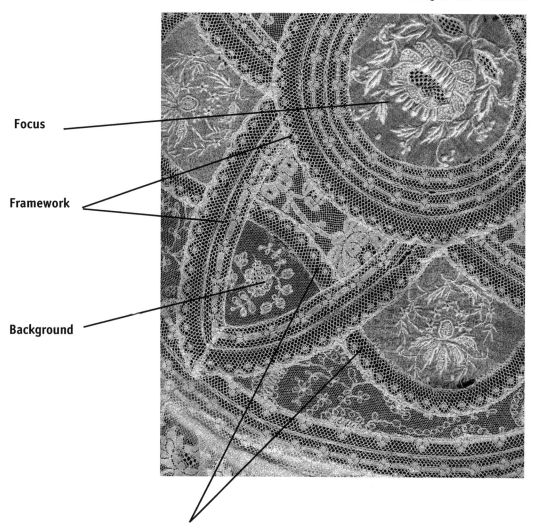

Subtle details like the way the edging flips direction as the curves change direction give movement to the design.

Ways of Planning Lace Patchworks

Template based patchworks
Complex frameworks of edgings that depict overlapping circles, ovals, squares and rectangles often form the base of lace patchworks.

The design often starts with a simple whitework round and builds from there. The most interesting templates overlap and interplay with each other, creating a unified and dynamic design.

Study as many patchworks as you can find. You soon will notice which templates are truly original, which are variations on a theme. Template-based designs were the most typical for circa-1920s commercial patchworks; made from what at the time were new materials. The makers could work from a template, and order as much material as needed for their designs.

Template-based designs are faster and easier to make because less thought and creativity goes into the arrangement of the lace. Using a template is an excellent way to start to learn how to make lace patchworks.

A center like a baseball diamond arranged around plate-sized whitework rounds was a particularly popular template for large patchworks. The bedspread above is shown in reverse on the opposite page. The "bases" all are identical, a clue that the bedspread was made from commercial all-new whitework.

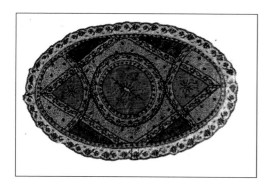

Looking at Lace Patchworks

Above : Patchwork tablecloth follows the same baseball-diamond template as the bedspread at left. Each of the "bases" in the tablecloth is different, with dense embroidery with needle lace inserts, suggesting they were originally vintage cap backs. The layout, workmanship, and other materials suggest the tablecloth was commercially made. More views of this patchwork are shown in the Gallery.

Opposite page and at right: Patchworks shown in reverse to emphasize their typical geometric templates.

Right: Strong cross of lace radiating from the center forms a skeleton for the patchwork shown in reverse. Each space is filled crazy-quilt style with other laces. Two sides have matching filet lace triangles with butterflies. For more views of this patchwork, see the Gallery.

Looking at Lace Patchworks

American folk-art lace patchworks typically were assembled around whatever favorite pieces the lacemaker found in her stash. This antimacassar, found in a Dallas, Texas area antique show, probably was assembled around the needle lace triangle at the top.

Opportunistic patchworks

Lace patchworks often were made up from recycled lace items. The patchwork-maker started with the lace objects at hand: a fan leaf, sometimes a handkerchief cut in quarters to obtain four symmetrical corners; perhaps whole doilies or a doily cut in half for half-rounds. The overall patchwork was then built around those objects.

A curve of lace may be recognized as part of a collar or the recycled edge of a large centerpiece. Opportunistic designs were typical in commemorative, artisanal or homemade lace patchworks, where favorite family pieces were recycled in tablecloths made as wedding presents or other gifts. Commercial opportunistic patchworks do show up, often as a hybrid between pieceworks, assembled from finished shaped lace pieces and true patchworks of cut lace bits.

Examples of an opportunistic commercial patchworks are is shown in the Gallery. See Connoisseur's Choice, Collector's Quarry, and Mother's Prize.

Looking at Lace Patchworks

Lappet or headdress set running down the center of the patchwork is the focus of this runner. Other pieces, including cut collars and round medallions radiate from that central item. The sophisticated plan, quantity and high quality of the handmade lace suggests the patchwork was commercially made.

More views of this patchwork are shown in the Gallery.

Materials

Each lace patchwork is an archeological dig. A single lace patchwork can include bits of lace from the reign of Louis XIV, nineteenth century Belgian and English lace, and twentieth century machine made yardage. This surprising range and variety is the joy and fascination of lace patchworks.

Those who are most comfortable identifying types of lace and separating handmade from machine will find the most valuable patchworks. To learn to identify a range of types of lace, get a good reference book for lace identification – such as the author's *Guide to Lace and Linens*.

The extremely rare patchworks include nineteenth century French cap backs and fine pieces of handmade lace. Template-based commercial patchworks are readily identified by the limited range of materials.

A good approach to looking at the materials is to check each aspect:

■ **Focus pieces**
First look for white-on-white embroideries. White-on-white embroidery is the focus in many European patchworks. French *fond du bonet*, is the most rare and valuable; a similar but simpler whitework appears in commercial patchworks.

Look for items embedded in the patchwork; perhaps a fan leaf, handkerchief section, round collar section or lappet. These signal interesting and often very valuable opportunisitic patchworks.

■ **Framework**
Look closely at the edgings and insertions that form the framework. Determine if they are handmade or machine made, and of what age and quality. Many of the template-based patchworks commercially produced for sale in the United States used the same assortment of edging and insertion laces.

■ **Background material**
Fine cotton embroidered net or other lace with an all-over pattern was the most frequently used background in commercially produced patchworks. Artisanal and American folk-art patchwork makers often filled in spaces with large plain net background areas with appliques of assorted lace motifs on top.

Looking at Lace Patchworks

Learning to recognize the differences between original vintage French fond du bonet, *above, and the simpler commercially produced version below is a key to becoming a connoisseur of Normandy Lace patchworks. Key differences are discussed on the following pages. Images are shown in the negative to emphasize lines and masses in the designs.*

Looking at Lace Patchworks

Classic French *fond du bonet*

Fine antique French embroideries with lace insertions and drawnwork are a rare and prized inclusion in lace pieceworks. Features that define them include:

- Dense designs with very large flowers.

- Heavily padded embroidery.

- Textural contrast of sanding or seed stitch and padded satin stitch.

- Cut holes in the design with insertions of lace are a highlight of the best quality *fond du bonet*.

The odd shapes of these insertions are a distinctive feature of real French *fond du bonet*. Note how the insertions conform to shapes of flower petals and leaves and enhance the overall embroidery design.

Vintage French fond du bonet *embroideries typically have large motifs, dense patterns, and wonderful lace inserts in the designs. The two designs at top left have inserts of needle lace.*

The large flower at bottom left has inserts of bobbin lace. Note how the pattern in the bobbin lace follows the direction of the hole it fills and enhances the overall design.

Looking at Lace Patchworks

Insertions of needle lace are perhaps the most attractive and best, but look also for insertions of other pieces of lace, including cut bits of handmade bobbin lace or machine made laces. Often these insertions were original to the embroidery; occasionally they may be replacing damaged needle lace.

This amazing and wonderful variety – no two ever seem to be alike – is the hallmark of true old hand work.

The examples of *fond du bonet* shown on these two pages all are part of the remarkable bedspread shown on page 40.

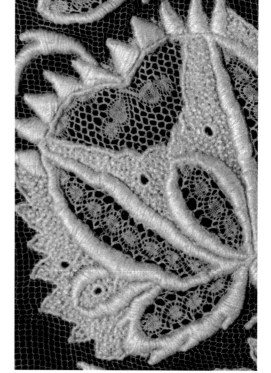

Top right: Needle lace inserts with a fabulous array of stitches that are shaped to enhance the design are the hallmark of the best French fond du bonet.

Bottom right: Inserts of bobbin lace or machine lace are not uncommon. This large flower with heavy satin and sanding stitches has been rescued from old fabric and applied to new machine net. The inserts, however, do appear to be original.

Looking at Lace Patchworks

Commercial whitework

The white-on-white embroideries included in the commercially made Normandy patchworks are lovely in their own right, just simpler than those from the original French cap backs. They differ from the "real" *fond du bonet* in several ways:

■ Designs are much simpler and "thinner." Simple groups of small flowers with fine trailing vines and tiny leaves are typical.

■ The old *fond du bonet* will have many large areas of sanding and other textural accents; the commercial versions use only satin stitch and occasional small, thin bits of sanding.

■ Flower centers may include a small accent of drawnwork; they rarely have needle lace inserts.

Above: two commercially produced whitework rounds with typical simple designs of thin, trailing vines, leaves, and little flowers.

Opposite page: Most of the commercially produced whitework was hand embroidered. Note the slight differences in the curves and the way ends of tendrils are finished off. The sanding stitch in each of the small leaves is worked at a slightly different angle and with a different number of stitches.

Thread in commercial whitework also is slightly heavier than that used in most of the original French fond du bonet.

Looking at Lace Patchworks

Some were machine embroideries done with the nineteenth century *handmachine*, a pantograph-guided sewing machine with many double-pointed needles. These machine embroideries often are nearly indistinguishable from hand embroidery.

To identify machine embroidery, look at the back, and compare similar motifs, or similar parts of motifs. Flower petals will have the same number of stitches, and the machine will jump from one petal to another at exactly the same point.

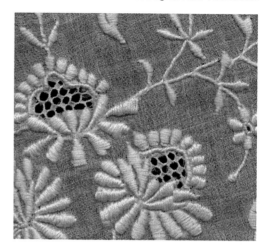

Commercial whitework flowers usually have only minimal drawnwork embellishment in the centers.

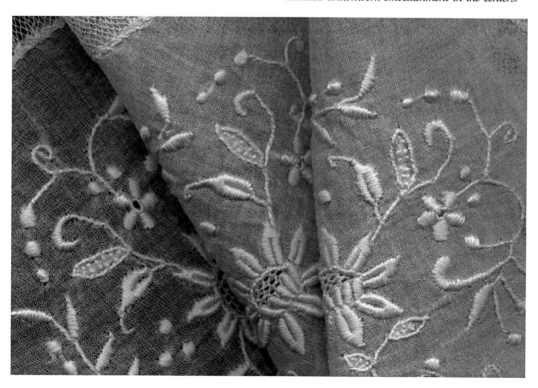

Looking at Lace Patchworks

Machine lace for background

A limited range of allover patterns of machine embroidery and other machine laces were very commonly used in commercial Normandy Lace patchworks.

Although they appear in so many of the commercial patchworks that they begin to seem commonplace, they were of superb quality. Made of fine cotton thread, they were very soft, supple, and with very graceful designs.

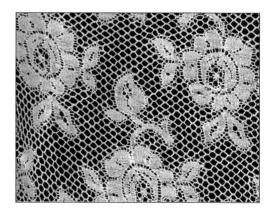

Typical machine laces for patchworks. Above, Leavers lace; at right and below, embroidered nets. All are shown about eighty percent actual size.

Looking at Lace Patchworks

Machine lace insertions and edgings

Machine yardage in the same design often was used in scallop edgings and insertions of different widths in the same piecework. Both the insertions and yardage typically had a draw thread on one side, and were used to form curves that encircle the whitework rounds.

Excellent quality machine imitations of Valenciennes, Mechlin, and Point de Paris, and other bobbin lace were typical.

Right and below right: Details from early 20th century commercial European lace patchwork shown on page 13.

Below: Machine lace edgings and insertions in a pattern very often found in commercial patchworks. Widths range from about two inches to an inch and a quarter.

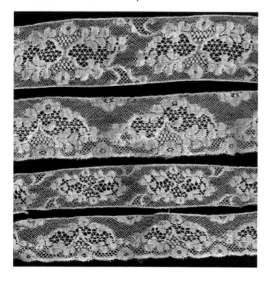

Judging Intrinsic Worth

What makes this piece special? That's the overall question that needs to be answered to determine how good a piece is, and what its intrinsic value is. What someone is willing to pay for it is a totally different thing, and often doesn't relate to the true intrinsic worth.

Each lace patchwork can be judged on design, materials, and condition. Those factors taken together determine rarity. Individual elements are evaluated and tallied, then the overall sum is considered.

The equation never is simple, because design and materials are so closely related. Each lace or embroidery fragment has a design and texture of its own; good patchwork designs consider and use that.

The importance of condition – damage to any specific element – will be related to how it affects the design, and how important or valuable that damaged patch of material or section of the whole may be.

Consider each element individually; then consider it again in relationship to others and to the whole of the patchwork.

Opposite page: This lace patchwork was the inspiration for this book. It was found by the author about 1980 in London's Camden Passage flea market. The condition of many of the individual pieces is poor; the overall spread however remains one of the most amazing collections of nineteenth century fond du bonet. A section of this bedspread is shown on page 11; details of fond du bonet from this bedspread are shown on pages 33, 34 and 35.

■ **Materials**
Quality of materials. Relationship of pattern of the lace material to the overall patchwork plan.

■ **Condition**

■ **Design**
Complexity
Coherence
Movement
Contrast

■ **Technique and workmanship**

■ **Rarity and Market Value**
Each category has its own rarities, related to design, materials, and condition.

Materials

Not only is this the finest quality fond du bonet, *the way it is cut out as an applique is extraordinary.*

Judge the patchwork by the quality of the individual pieces of lace, how well they blend, and how suitable they are for use in the specific design. Not only are the materials related to the design, they are related to condition. Damaged commercial background or embroidery rounds are fairly interchangeable in commercial patchworks. French cap backs are one-of-a kind, often define the design, and may be irreplaceable.

Appropriateness of materials to the design.

■ How does the design of the material play into the overall design of the piece?

■ Is the texture of materials in the patchwork suitable for the design?

■ Do the patterns in the lace blend and contrast with each other, and do they fit with the overall design of the patchwork?

Patchworks within patchworks add to the joy of discovery in Normandy Lace. The section of Brussels Mixed lace already was a combination of Duchesse bobbin lace and Point de Gaze needle lace before the handkerchief corner was cut up and inserted in the patchwork.

Finished edges on all sides of the triangle say the filet lace butterfly was designed as an insertion.

Judging Intrinsic Worth

Quality of materials
Look for handmade materials of good design. Especially desirable are:

- Real French *fond du bonet*.

- Mechlin, Valenciennes, and Bucks Point bobbin lace insertions and edgings.

- Point de Gaze, Duchesse, and other good handmade craft laces like filet or Battenberg.

- Curiosities, such as handmade 17th and 18th century laces.

- Laces with animals, figures, birds.

- Good quality all cotton laces.

Section of a tablecloth coontaining a variety of handmade laces, including Point de Gaze, Duchesse, Brussels Mixed, and other bobbin and needle laces. The three foot by nine foot tablecloth sold at auction for $5,462 in June of 2003 by Neil Auction house in New Orleans, Louisiana.

Design

The overall design should be complex enough to hold interest, and reveal something new each time it is inspected; but not be so busy that it is confusing.

Design of the overall patchwork always is a marriage between the overall plan for the patchwork, and the patterns and texture of the materials that make it up.

Taste in design may be very personal, but consider certain basic factors, and perhaps your tastes will broaden. The design of patchworks is closely related to the materials used to make it, and the skill and care in the workmanship. Reject pieces that have boring designs. Treasure pieces with good design.

Characteristics of good design

Regardless of whether the patchwork is opportunistic or template-based, certain characteristics define a good design:

■ **Complexity.** Is the overall design interesting enough to look at more than once? Do you see it all the first time, or do you discover something new at each viewing?

■ **Coherence.** Does anything tie the overall design together? Does the framework of insertions or edgings overlap, interlink or otherwise unify the design?

■ **Movement.** Do elements of the design draw your eye around the design and give the design life?

■ **Contrast.** Contrast can be subtle or glaring, but there should be enough of a difference in patterns of the individual pieces so that an overall design emerges. Is there significant, sufficient contrast in density, complexity, and texture between the adjacent laces to establish the focus, the background and the connectors?

Opposite page: Design of this centerpiece or placemat is an unusual hybrid between opportunistic and template-based. Side triangles intrude on the center, and bring the design together and make our eyes move at the same time. Patchwork maker thought carefully about how the designs of the lace pieces complement the overall design of the patchwork.

Thes placemat was part of a large set of several placemats and doilies. See Vive le Difference in the Gallery.

Judging Intrinsic Worth

Part of a commercially-produced bedspread illustrating the relationship of materials and design. The stripe of the background has too much pattern of its own, and fights with the rest of the design.

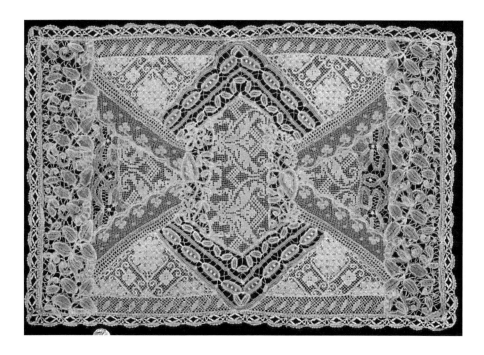

Judging Intrinsic Worth

Overall good design:

This long table runner is an interesting hybrid between opportunisitc, or a patchwork built around the round whitework pieces, and template-based, with a framework of lace edgings and insertions.

Especially interesting are the two curves with slightly different radii at the top and bottom. These create an interesting movement to the overall design. Choice of patterns in the laces provide nice contrast and balance.

Overall bad design (opposite page):
The overall framework of the plan is boring: everything is obvious at first glance. There is no interplay, no movement, no grace.

There is no contrast between the background and the connecting pieces; the overall plan is not visible.

Materials are nice but predictable machine made laces seen in hundreds of commercial pieces. This is a piece that might well be taken apart, and the materials re-used in a more interesting patchwork.

Judging Intrinsic Worth

Overall bad design:
Design looks like five large cookies on a tray. Everything is visible at first glance, with no interaction or relationship.

Materials are nice tape lace; decent but not exciting quality.

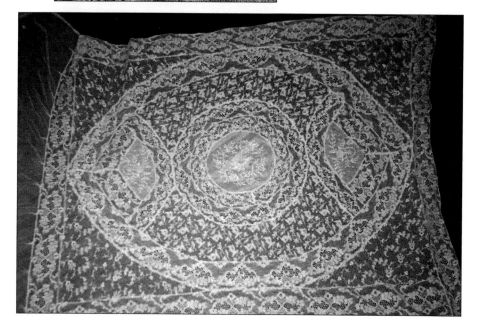

47

Technique and Workmanship

In even the best quality lace patchworks, the sewing almost invariably was nothing more than whip or overcast stitches, and rather loose at that. Only very rarely is a commercial piece found that has been stitched together by machine with a zig-zag stitch.

The technique and workmanship more often relates to the layout, getting the geometry right, getting the proper mitering of corners, and planning the best arrangement of insertions. The geometry does not necessarily have to be perfect. Sometimes just the right bit of lopsidedness makes the overall design more charming; too much and it is just sloppy.

Trimming the edges along the seams on the back side also affects the overall framework and design of the patchwork. Usually, the seams are trimmed to about a quarter to an eighth of an inch. This slightly blurs the edge, and leaves raw edges that inevitably start to fray, but that's how it was done.

When an extremely wide margin was left – perhaps a half inch or more – the design on the front is affected. The overall design is slightly blurred. These exceptionally wide margins sometimes indicate a piece has been replaced.

The simple geometric design of this centerpiece leaves no room for sloppy workmanship. What could be a charming little "Easter egg" design is lost because the lopsided shapes call attention to themselves, and obscure the overall design of interlocking ovals.

Judging Intrinsic Worth

Occasionally a commercially made patchwork is found that has been stitched together by machine. Whitework here also is machine embroidered. Back view shows the typical ridge of the bobbin thread.

Machine lace backround was not trimmed close to the seam, and overlaps the filet lace at top left and bottom. This muddies the line of the design.

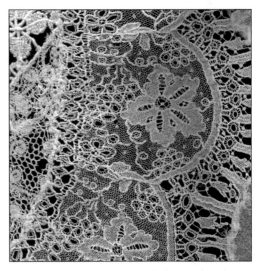

Whitework is trimmed closely, then rolled and overcast along the seam. This cleanly defines the lines that create the framework and shape of the patchwork.

Seam at left above is trimmed close to the edge, and overcast to define the line of the little rounds. Other seams are trimmed closely enough to hide the edge behind a dense part of the edge.

Condition

Assessing the condition of a lace patchwork is crucial. It is impossible to predict what kinds of lace will be found, or what age the pieces might be. Seventeenth century handmade laces might be adjacent to twentieth century machine yardage. It was not uncommon for laces of questionable condition to be included, because the point of making the patchwork was to keep treasured old pieces visible.

The types and amounts of damage are important to note, as well as where the damage is located. Some types of damage are easy to repair. The patchworks were originally put together with loose whip stitches, and damaged pieces often can be easily removed. How easily they can be replaced depends on how crucial the piece is to the design, and whether a suitable replacement is available.

When considering a piece to buy, do a little quick mathematics. Fine old patchworks were made of cotton and linen lace. Replacing cotton insertions will cost a minimum of $2 per yard. Pretty scalloped yardage for the ruffle around the edge will cost between $5 and $10 per yard, if enough yardage can be found. A tablecloth could easily require 10 yards – a hundred dollar investment if it can be found at all.

When evaluating a damaged piece to sell, be realistic about the cost of fixing damaged areas.

How to look for damage

Patchworks are dazzling, and damage often is hidden in the complex patterns. Following the checklist of focus pieces, background, and framework lace is a useful way to be sure to inspect all aspects of the patchwork, and find all the damage.

Search the back of the piece for tulle patches. Decades ago, the classic technique for "mending" Normandy patchworks was to support damaged lace by stitching a piece of tulle behind it. Finding tulle stitched to the back of any lace piece usually indicates holes at best, dry rot at worst.

Many lace patchwork designs were symmetrical. Look for matching pieces in the symmetry when assessing the condition of any patchwork. If the filet butterfly in one corner is dry rotted, chances are the three in the other corners are as well. If a particular line of insertion lace in the framework is deteriorating, look for similar lace in other parts of the framework.

Crazy patchwork may have matching pieces, or fragments cut from the same item, scattered throughout the patchwork. When you find one problem piece, start a search for others that match. Consider also that what originally was symmetrical patchwork has become a "crazy" with replacement parts!

What to look for

- **Separating seams.** Carefully inspect all the seams. It is typical for them to be coming apart. Seams are easy and fast to fix if the edges of the lace have not begun to shred. The repair process becomes much more complex and expensive if they have.

- **Stains.** Staining sometimes means the piece will need to be replaced. Patchworks should not be bleached or treated with whitening agents like Oxyclean or Biz. These damage the already old and fragile laces, and often destroy them entirely.

- **Damaged background pieces.** Plain net and mesh are difficult repair and need to be replaced. Patterned background pieces offer places to camoflage or hide repairs.

- **Damaged framework lace.** Beware of dry rot in the insertion laces that form the skeleton of the piecework. These are expensive and difficult to replace.

- **Focus pieces.** Significant damage to the focus pieces, especially fragile white-on-white embroidery significantly reduces the overall value.

- **Damaged whitework.** Splits and tears in the whitework, especially old *fond du bonet*, are very difficult and expensive to repair or replace.

Slight shredding around the edge of the whitework often can be repaired. A hole or stain in the center of the whitework is a big problem. The fabric is so fine there is no where to hide the darning or patch.

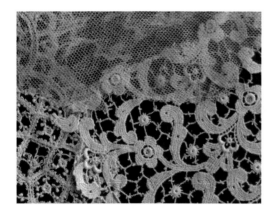

Beware of tulle patches on the back of patchworks. They were a popular way of "repairing" damaged and often signal dry-rotted lace pieces in patchworks.

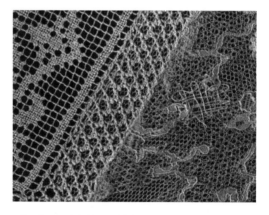

The darned hole and blurred or odd appearance of the lace suggests serious damage, probably dry rot, which needed the support of tulle.

Judging Intrinsic Worth

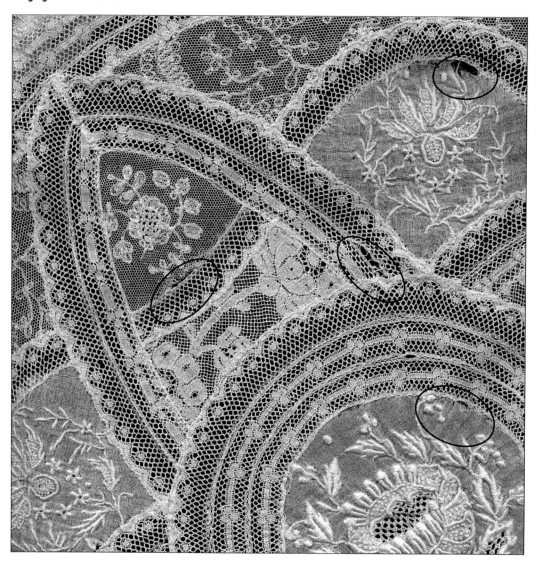

Split seam at right is the easiest flaw to repair. The seam simply is stitched back together.

Frayed edge at left is more difficult. The edges cannot be pulled together to resew – the stress will pull them apart and tear more of the net.

It is possible but not easy to repair damage to the edge of the whitework. Any holes or frays in the center of the whitework are a very serious problem, difficult and expensive to repair.

Rarity and Market Value

The most rare Normandy Lace patchworks are those with the best and most unusual designs and the best handmade lace in the best condition.

In general, commercial, template-based patchworks from the early 20th century are the most plentiful. Opportunistic and artisanal folk-art designs are more rare.

Patchworks with original French *fond du bonet* are rare. Original large patchworks in good condition are exceptionally rare because the weight of the embroidery was too heavy for the fabric even at the time it was made. The fabric inevitably cracks and shreds around the embroidery.

 Commercial European patchworks with template-based designs are the type most often found. Within that category, however, there are exceptionally well designed pieces, with unusual machine made laces.

Opportunistic designs arranged around unique handmade pieces, such as a fan leaf, collar, lappet, or handkerchief are quire rare. Really well designed pieces made with good handmade lace are exceptionally rare.

Greek Lace Mosaics were made for a very short time, in a small area, and are very rare.

American artisanal pieces are relatively rare to begin with. Being able to identify the maker adds to the rarity.

Rarity alone does not make mean a piece will bring a high market price. So few appreciate and understand lace patchworks it is difficult to get a good price for good pieces. Simply based on the laws of supply and demand, however, the most common pieces can provide enough for the relatively small audience that is knowledgeable about lace patchworks.

Gallery

Looking thoughtfully at many lace patchworks is the best way to learn what is good, what is not so good, what is rare and what is ordinary. It also is a great way to get ideas to copy.

Categories were suggested earlier in this book: Classic French with original *fond du bonet*, European commercial derived from those original French pieces; American artisanal, Greek lace mosaics. The reality in the market place is never quite so tidy.

Many times the design clearly is template based, sometimes opportunistic, designed around a few key pieces. Often it is a blend of more than one type.

Nevertheless, using the features of the various categories as a checklist is a useful way to look for clues in the design, materials, and technique. Most of all, using a checklist is a good way to see all that the lace patchwork has to offer.

Identify

■ Materials
- Are the materials handmade or machine?

- Is there any *fond du bonet*?

- Is it classic old French, with fabulous needle lace and drawnwork instertions, or a simplified commercial version?

- Is there a wide variety of handmade and machine laces, dating from a wide range of decades, or are all the materials from one time period?

■ Design
- Is it template-based, with a geometric skeleton established with narrow lace insertions and edgings?

- Is it opportunistic, with an overall design arranged around a few key pieces?

Judge

■ Design
Quirkiness and originality are the trump virtues that sets the work of one maker apart. Look for an interesting relationship between pattern and texture in the materials and the overall design. Look for complexity, coherence, movement and flow.

■ Materials
Look for an unusual range of styles and ages in the materials. Look especially for high-quality handmade laces from the nineteenth century or earlier.

■ Condition
Inspect all seams and materials carefully. Especially if the laces came from a wide range of ages and sources, look for damage to the lace itself.

■ Technique
How neatly were the seams stitched and trimmed? Was the design carefully shaped?

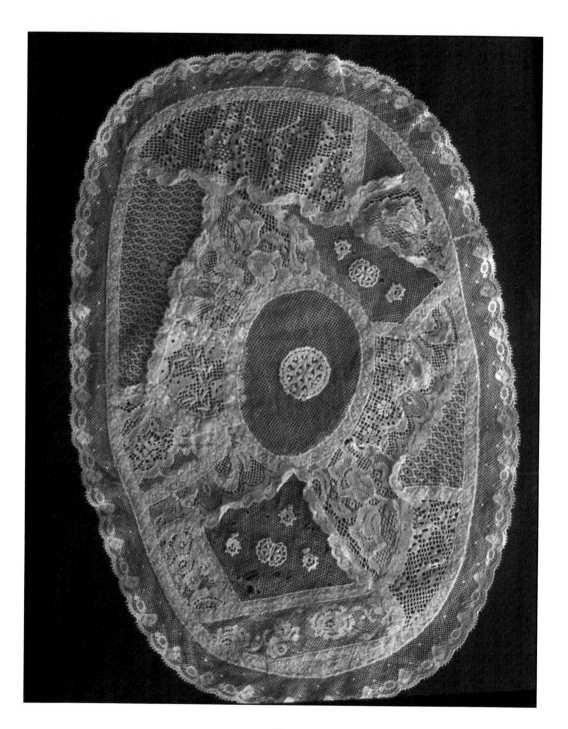

Simple Gifts

'Tis the gift to be simple,'Tis the gift to be free,
'Tis the gift to come down where we ought to be,

And when we find ourselves in the place just right,
It will be in the valley of love and delight.

When true simplicity is gained,
to bow and to bend, we shan't be ashamed.

To turn, turn, will be our delight,
'Til by turning, turning, we come round right.

Joseph Brackett, Jr.
A Shaker Elder, 1846

Whoever made this little patchwork understood the simple delight of playing with lace, with complete honesty and absolutely no fear of lace police.

It is only by working by eye rather than with any rulers, compasses or drawing aids, and relying on instinct for design can something this simply charming be made. And yet the maker has instinctively hit every one of the rules of good design.

The maker balanced and harmonized the design with matching bits of the same lace in alternate places in the patchwork.

There is complexity and movement to the design, partly achieved by the slightly crooked quality of the oval in the center and the oval outside edge, and the odd shapes of the patches. All of the materials are rather common machine made laces. None of them ever appear in the commercial European patchworks.

Finally, the little ruffle of lace that hides the rough edges gives a wonderful texture.

The condition is not excellent. One of the faux-filet laces patches alongside the center appears to be a replacement. The plain net side pieces are rather badly damaged, but it would be a pity to replace or mend them. This is one case where the damage also is true to the originality and simplicity of the whole.

American Artisanal patchwork at left is about 12 inches by about 9 inches.

Gallery

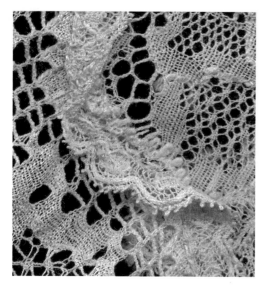

Slightly ruffled edging was whip-stitched on to cover the rough edges where lace pieces meet and overlap.

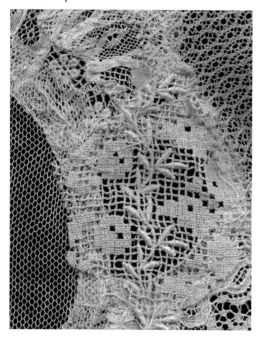

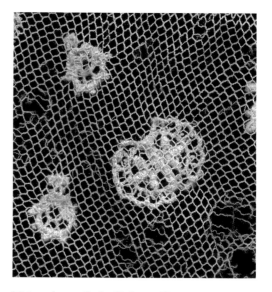

Net underneath the little appliques appears to be in perfect condition, a clue that they were original and not put on to patch holes.

Back view shows patchwork is very rudely stitched together, with most seams left untrimmed. This bit of machine filet lace appears somewhat heavier, darker in color, and out of sync, and may be a repair, but the crude construction makes it difficult to know.

Gallery

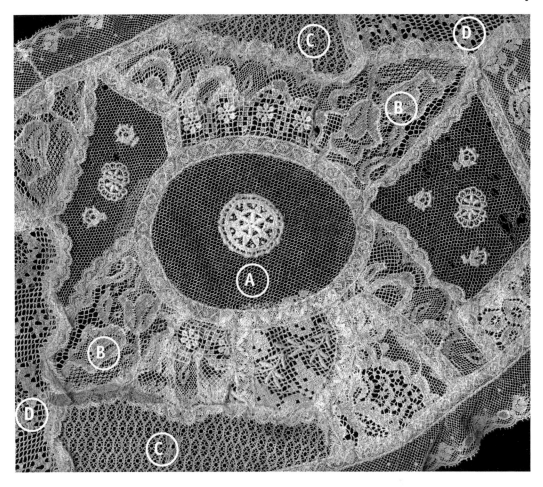

There is a rudimentary symmetry in the overall patchwork. Groups of patches starting with A, and going counterclockwise around the center have a similar shape.

This overall design could have been instinctive, or planned on the part of the maker.

A: *Slightly lopsided but pleasing to the eye: the center motif is just right.*

B, C, D: *Matching materials in different shapes in opposite places give a coherence and balance to the overall design.*

Unfinished Symphony

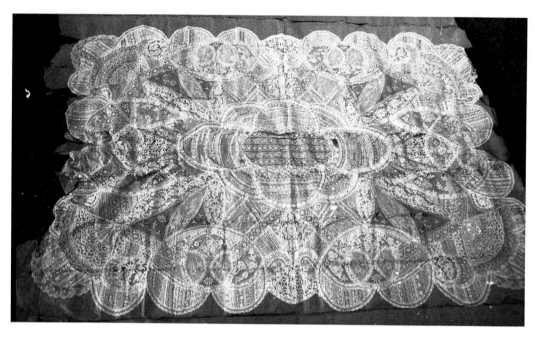

Patchwork is a large double bedspread size, American Artisanal, and begun by an unknown maker in Texas about 1930-1940.

Pieceworks that were started but never finished tell the story of how these patchworks were assembled, and give us a glimpse into the past to see the varied materials someone had gathered up in years past.

The value of these can be as varied as the materials and designs that make them up.

To finish them and use them, leave them as-is for future generations to marvel over, or to harvest the trove of materials to make a patchwork of one's own – all are questions to consider.

Lace that has spent seventy or more years stitched to acidic paper may well be dry rotted. Certainly leaving it on the paper is not healthy for the lace. Plus the piece is not usable. One possibility is to carefully document the unfinished piece with photography, then finish off the piece.

Assigning a value to each patchwork will depend on the same factors we've used for all judging: How good is the design, how good are the materials, how well do they fit together? Finally, an assessment of condition.

Each of the lace pieces should be looked at for deterioration. Especally of concern are machine laces made by the "chemical" or "aetz" process. These were made by machine embroidering the lace over a substrate which was then chemically dissolved away. Over many years, these in particular tend to deteriorate. Spending those years attached to acidic paper increases the likelihood they will be crumbling.

Opposite page: Patchwork still mounted on the original brown butcher paper. The delight of American artisanal patchworks is the variety and unique style of each patchwork maker. The overall design of this patchwork is defined by lines of narrow lace insertions and edgings. The spaces often are filled with strips of lace or crazy patchworks made by stitching together little bits of lace.

Many of the spaces are filled with strips of lace insertions and edgings stitched together. Quite a few spaces have chemical lace as the filling. These are especially likely to deteriorate over time.

Texas Treasures

Blanche Phillippi Cavender was the ideal lady to make patchworks of vintage lace in the 1920s. She made four impressive patchworks tablecloths, each a wedding gift for one of her children.

The golden age of lacemaking still was a fresh memory, and any snippet of old lace was too good to throw away. She was a society lady in the Dallas, Texas area when oil, cattle and banking made it a prosperous and exciting place to live.

Blanche was an artist and a musician, and very active in music and the arts in the Dallas area.

Vintage lace from fashions and household decorating would have been a natural part of her life. Through her position in the community and activity in the arts she undoubtedly had friends who happily added to her collection of lace, happy to have their unused vintage lace used in such a celebratory way.

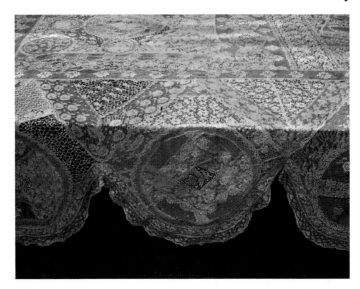

The delight of American Artisanal patchworks is the unique style developed by each maker.

Opposite page, top: Blanche Phillippi Cavender shown with one of her four children. Blanche made four Normandy Lace patchwork tablecloths as wedding gifts, one for each of her children. It was probably just a few years later that Blanche made a tablecloth for this daughter.

Opposite page, below: center of one of Blanche Phillipi Cavender's lace patchwork tablecloths.

Each of the Cavender's tablecloths was tinted a deep ecru, possibly with the "powdered ochre" which was fashionable in the 1920s and 1930s. That, plus age, has taken a toll on some of the areas of the patchwork.

Mary Martin's Mother's Tablecloth

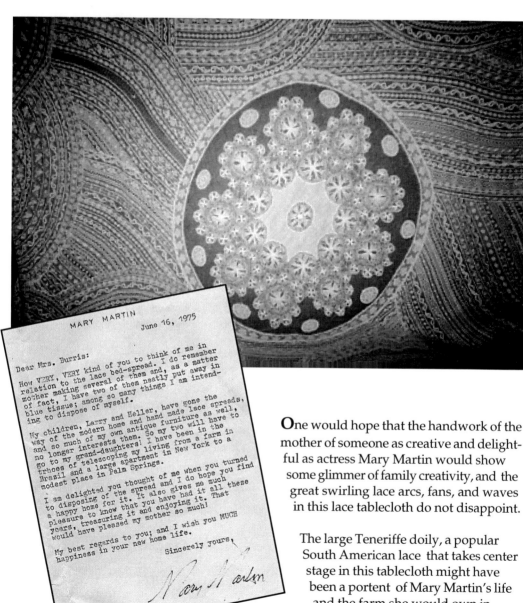

MARY MARTIN
June 16, 1975

Dear Mrs. Burris:

How VERY, VERY kind of you to think of me in relation to the lace bed-spread. I do remember mother making several of them and, as a matter of fact, I have two of them neatly put away in blue tissue; among so many things I am intending to dispose of myself.

My children, Larry and Heller, have gone the way of the modern home and hand made lace spreads, and so much of my own antique furniture as well, no longer interests them. So my two will have to go to my grand-daughters! I have been in the trhoes of telescoping my living from a farm in Brazil and a large apartment in New York to a modest place in Palm Springs.

I am delighted you thought of me when you turned to disposing of the spread and I do hope you find a happy home for it. It also gives me much pleasure to know that you have had it all these years, treasuring it and enjoying it. That would have pleased my mother so much!

My best regards to you; and I wish you MUCH happiness in your new home life.

Sincerely yours,
Mary Martin

One would hope that the handwork of the mother of someone as creative and delightful as actress Mary Martin would show some glimmer of family creativity, and the great swirling lace arcs, fans, and waves in this lace tablecloth do not disappoint.

The large Teneriffe doily, a popular South American lace that takes center stage in this tablecloth might have been a portent of Mary Martin's life and the farm she would own in Brazil. The letter at left was written

Gallery

Except for a centerpiece of Teneriffe lace appliqued to a plain net, almost the entire tablecloth is made up of yards and yards and yards of machine lace insertions and edgings, stitched together into great swirls. Tablecloth measures about 64 inches by 106 inches.

just over a year after her husband and manager Richard Halliday died at their farm in Brazil.

The tablecloth predates all that, reaching back probably to the late 1920s, before she became famous. About 1930, at the age of almost seventeen, she married Benjamin Hagman. The son mentioned in the letter is actor Larry Hagman. Just a few years later, in the early 1930s they were divorced and she started a dancing school in Weatherford. The Mrs. Burris addressed in the letter is a daughter of the friend who obtained it from Mary Martin's mother. She was a student in that dancing school. The tablecloth shown above remains in their family.

Bows and Buttons

Condition alone should have relegated this small patchwork to the scrap heap. Not only was it stained and smelling of dust and perfumes trying to cover up the mustiness, but one side was entirely falling off.

Follow the connoisseur's checklist, however, and consider design, materials, and workmanship before condition. There may be some redeeming value.

Take a close look – hard to do when the mustiness tells you to keep it at arm's length – and this little centerpiece fairly screams "copy that!"

The centerpiece is a classic American Artisanal patchwork, and probably was built up around the tiny center round of bobbin lace. Design and technique tricks are in the corners, in the way the frame is built up, and in filling large side spaces.

The charming bows were a favorite 1930s design trick, and a great way to fill space on a large area of plain net. The little button motif salvaged from another piece of embroidery neatly hides the messy center where the lace crosses.

The design makes good use of chemical lace motifs, which were made by embroidering a design in a lock stitch on a substrate, which was later chemically dissolved away, releasing the lock-stitched embroidery as a free piece of lace. The lock-stitched embroidery motifs can be cut out with relatively clean edges that do not unravel.

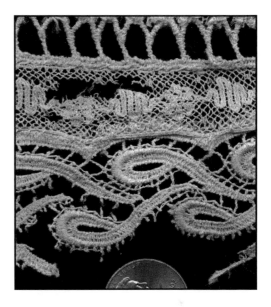

The shredded lace insert and the shattered edging scream dry rot, a terminal condition. The quaint centerpiece, however, did survive a washing without disintegrating, and can live on life support long enough to show off a few ideas worth copying.

Opposite page: American Artisanal patchwork, about 11 inches by 17 inches, by an unknown maker in Texas circa 1930s.

Gallery

There is one major drawback to using vintage chemical lace: it is notoriously fragile. While the dense clothwork areas may still hold up fairly well, very fine connecting bars can be expected to fray and break.

Above: Square flowers were cut out and stitched in to form the corners, and another cut out leaf extends in to cover what would be an unatractive join of the ball-and-pillar edging that forms the inside of the frame.

Right back view: The center of each side is decorated with a cut out chemical lace motif.

A narrow lace insertion was folded and stitched to the plain net to form a decorative bow. A reverse view emphasizes the folds. A cut out round of embroidery covers the center like a button.

Rose Anne's Round

Doily, about eight inches around, origin unknown

We can never be certain where a piece was made, but clues can suggest when it was home made and when it was commercially made. This little round includes some nice handmade lace and a nice little piece of whitework embroidery in the center. How it was stitched together makes a strong case for a home made piece. Crude but clever tucks position the eyelet motifs to fit within the curves. Lace in the center is handmade Valenciennes, but salvaged bits and scraps seamed together.

Gallery

Left, detail below: The many seams in the center round are something to wonder about.

Little scraps of handmade Valenciennes bobbin lace, with no finished edge at the top were cobbled together to surround the whitework center. The cut edge is whip stitched to the edge of the fabric.

However crudely stitched, there appears to be a very specific reason for this tuck. The weave of the cloth changes direction at the seam. Without this tuck and the one at the top the eyelet motifs would not fit within the curved space.

Gallery

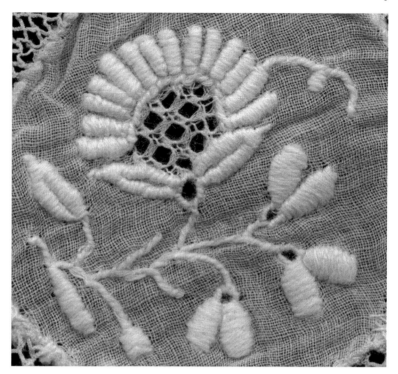

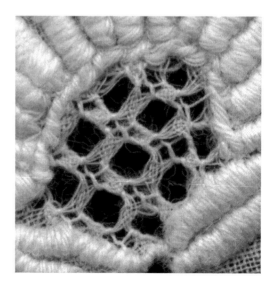

Little whitework flower in the center was salvaged and reused in this patchwork. It is simple and small enough that the design might be salvaged and copied and used again in a new patchwork. The drawnwork center is exceptionally pretty. Pattern shown about 125% actual size.

71

Second Hand Rose

Dense embroidery gives the rose a sculptural quality; contrast with the fine lace edging makes a spectacular display. Doily is about 8 1/2 inches in diameter.

Recycled, but what a rose! Originally embroidered on fine muslin, most likely as a cap back, this rose has been precisely trimmed from its original fabric and restitched onto a net. Even though it has been regrounded, the embroidery is rare enough that the doily would still be quite valuable.

The edging also is remarkable: it is fine handmade eighteenth English Bucks Point bobbin lace.

Square open mesh behind the rose contrasts nicely with the smaller, rounder mesh of the lace edge.

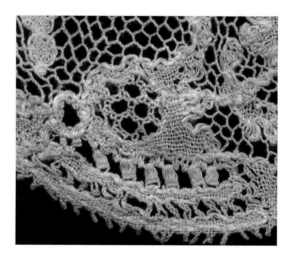

Thread manipulations reveal that the outside lace is handmade, likely English Bucks Point bobbin lace.

Forever and a Day

Doily from the 1920s defines "too good to throw away." Bits of vintage whitework less than an inch across were recycled into a patchwork. Little doily is actually a mere four inches in diameter.

Gallery

Endlessly recycled bits and pieces of vintage whitework, treasured and too good to throw away, appear in little doilies inserted in decorative glass-and-brass dresser and boudoir trays in the 1920s. These little patchworks with tiny bits of old French whitework are not uncommon flea-market finds today.

Enough similar pieces show up in antique shops and flea market to suggest they were made commercially, likely sold already in the little round or oval glass trays.

Typically the doilies are in poor condition, having spent decades pressed under glass in musty conditions.

Nevertheless, they are quaint rembrances of a colorful era, and testimony to a time when fine embroidery was still recognized, and even the littlest bits of frayed whitework were prominently displayed.

How many times the little whitework bit in the center has been recycled we can only guess. Very likely this is at least the second go-around: why else would the whitework be backed with net, instead of applied directly to the center patch?

The stitching technique is rather crude. The whitework bit has been attached to the net with large irregular stitches; the surrounding machine lace is stitched partly above and partly below the whitework center.

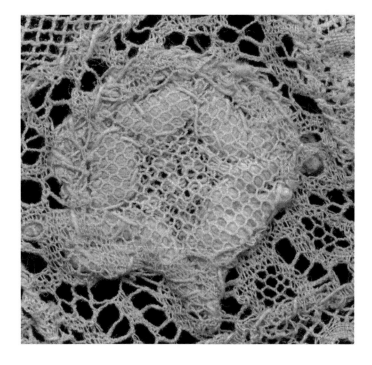

Emily's Missing Masterpieces

Each American artisan lace patchwork maker had a distinctive style. Although actual patchworks made by Emily Teagle have yet to surface, her style is readily apparent from an undated newspaper clipping from the *Oakland* (California) *Tribune*. The patchworks that appear in the photograph, along with another photograph of her collection of motifs, suggest that she favored overall designs that feature large expanses of tulle or net with appliques of interesting lace motifs.

Tribune Parade photo by Lonnie Wilson, reprinted with the permission of the Oakland (CA) Tribune

Emily Teagle is shown stitching on a lace patchwork in an undated newspaper clipping. Other material in the clipping suggest it was some time in about the 1950s.

According to the article, Teagle learned to make lace patchworks while she was living in the Dallas-Fort Worth area of Texas. Althought she probably was making lace patchworks at about the same time as Blanche Phillipi Cavendar (see page 62) and Mary Martin's Mother (see page 64) her style was different.

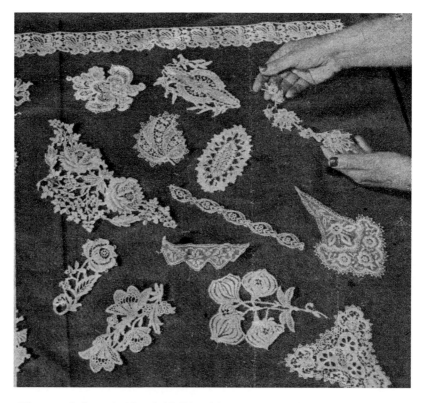

Photograph from Oakland (California) Tribune *articles gives us a glimpse into Emily Teagle's workshop, and some clues as to what materials she favored for her lace patchworks. Almost all of the laces pictured here appear to be machine made by the chemical or aetz process.*

Chemical laces were machine embroidered, and make great cut-outs. Most likely, many of the motifs appliqued onto net on the large patchworks shown in the other picture are chemical lace as well.

Jane's Gift

Patchwork is a template-based commercial European boudoir pillow. About 23 inches across, with a fine batiste button-back. Probably circa 1930.

Gallery

This lovely patchwork arrived unannounced in my mail, a gift from Jane Dilks. An attached note explained the poor condition made it unusable, probably unrepairable. Perhaps, she suggested, one of my mending classes could have some fun with it, and in any case, perhaps some one would learn something from it.

It is an absolutely typical commercially made European lace patchwork of the 1920s or 1930s. Working from a template or pattern, and filling in the blanks with available newly made lace and embroidery, a boudoir pillow such as this could easily have been made in a day.

This should not be dismissed, however, as a lesser-quality item. The materials all were fine cotton of a quality no longer made today. Plus there are indeed many things to be learned from this damaged piece.

The shredding whitework, the unraveled seams, and the holes in the Valenciennes edging all could be repaired. The repair work is detailed in the "Living With Lace Patchworks" section in this book.

Use it also as a benchmark for the design in template-based patchworks. The entwined laces provide interesting possibilites for a template.

Mentally erase the filling laces and embroideries, and visualize the skeleton that forms the basis for the patchwork.

This is a great pattern to copy for home-made patchworks today. Note how the direction of the lace insertion is reversed when the curves change direction. This makes the lace easier to shape, and also makes the design more interesting.

Whitework Wonderland

The bedspread, about 64 inches by 90 inches, is one of a pair. Also part of the set are boudoir pillows, shown on the following pages.

Whitework embroidery is the main event in this commercially made bedspread. This is a slight variation from the usual design of commercially produced patchwork. It also is rather unusual to have only one type of background lace.

Imagine the 1920s or 1930s glamour of a bedroom filled with lace. This bedspread is one of a set of nine similar boudoir pieces: the pair of bedspreads and seven pillow covers – two heart shaped, two round, and three oval.

There are some variations in each of the pieces, but the similarities are unmistakable. Each focuses on crescent-shaped whitework surrounded with a narrow

Gallery

The rounds are superb imitations of the original fond du bonet cap backs; the exaggerated shape of the crescents seem to be designs specifically to fit the design of the bedspread.

edging of lace. More lace, all a similar pattern of machine Valenciennes or Mechlin with large floral or leaf designs, is neatly centered to highlight the best parts of the lace designs in all the background spaces.

The lace in the bedspread is all machine made, but of very fine cotton. It is soft, supple, and of unusually fine quality. The edge flounce is almost a foot deep. Machine lace of this delicacy is not made today; the value of the flounce alone is well over ten dollars per yard.

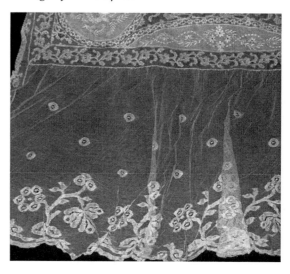

Gallery

Each of the boudoir pillows has a different design of lace ruffle, but each carefully imitates a classic nineteenth century handmade lace: Valenciennes, Mechlin, and Alencon. All the machine lace is of superb quality unmatched today.

The great number of coordinated pieces attests to a thriving industry somewhere in France in the first half of the twentieth century. Such a collection of coordinated pieces is a decorator's dream today. Because all of the lace was new when the patchworks were assembled, it is still strong and very usable today.

Heart shaped pillow, about 17 inches by 18 inches, was one of a pair.

Gallery

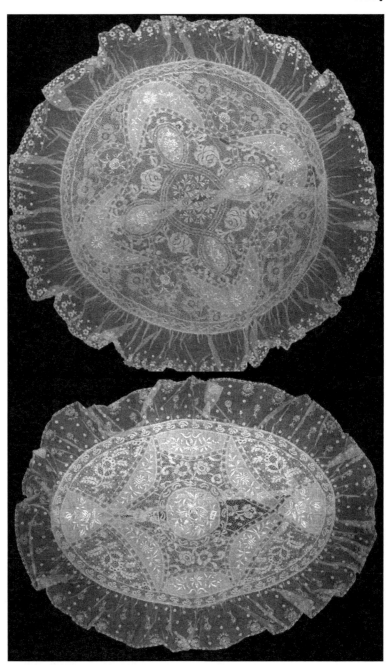

Round boudoir pillow cover, 23 inches across, is one of a pair. One of the pillow shams has a "Made in France" label.

Oval boudoir pillow, 17 inches by 23 inches, was one of three.

Quartet

Set of four matching doilies, each a slightly different size or shape, all made with the same machine-made laces and a similar geometric pattern tells us there was certainly a commercial industry somewhere. The creamy yellow color suggests they might date to the 1930s, when that color was especially popular.

The market value is minimal: almost all the doilies have some damage. All the seams are stitched together by machine, with a zig-zag stitch, making it is almost impossible to take the patchworks apart to recycle the still-good lace pieces.

They can continue to be pleasant, usable doilies as long as a perfume bottle or jewelry box can be positioned to cover the holes and stains.

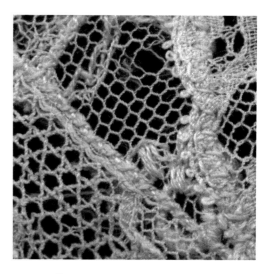

Seams all are machine-stitched with a zig-zag stitch.

Back view of the embroidery shows the embroidery was done with a machine that used a conventional double thread, a top thread and a bottom bobbin thread; not a nineteenth century handmachine, which stitched with a single thread.

Collector's Quarry

Like a remarkable archeological dig, this long table runner yields an array of vintage fashion items. Very likely it was formed around the long center line, which is a mid nineteenth century set of lappets. Shaped like a necktie with medallion-like oval ends, lappets were worn, pouffed and pinned, as headdresses or hair ornaments in the nineteenth century. When that fashion passed, they were endlessly recycled and often cut up. That this set survives in a patchwork is remarkable.

Also impressive is the variety and quality of the hand and machine made laces included in the patchwork.

This patchwork has it all: design, technique and workmanship, fine quality materials, and a remarkable relationship between the materials and the design. If it remains in excellent condition, wherever this patchwork goes off in the world it should be a collector's prize.

Table runner is 48 inches long and 20 inches wide. Oval medallions of Bucks Point bobbin lace form the centerline of the runner. Patchwork is opportunistic, designed around a long Point de Gaze needle lace lappet, or headdress streamer. (A negative image on page 31 emphasizes the lines.) Note the curious corner treatment. We will never know if there was not enough of the Duchesse bobbin lace to completely surround the runner, or if the designer chose to use two different laces as an accent to make the patchwork more interesting.

Gallery

Starting from the top left: handmade English Bucks Point bobbin lace medallion; v-shaped surround is formed by a bobbin lace insertion. Handmade filet lace fills in the background in the top section. An insertion of handmade Valenciennes bobbin lace and a wide border of handmade Duchesse bobbin lace finish off the edge.

Gallery

Above: Section of a tape lace collar with fine filling stitches curves from top left corner. Whitework embroidery at the right is machine made, but of superb quality.

Right: The fillings in the flower provide an excellent imitation of needle lace fillings. The thread manipulations, however, do not include any buttonhole stitches, but instead are the nervous, slightly hazy blatt stitch typical of embroidery machines. The use of such insertions in machine embroidery was a slow and complex process, and is no longer done.

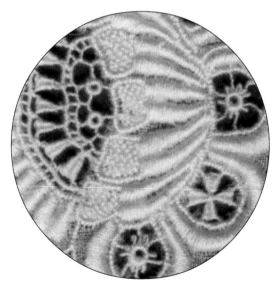

Dresser scarf, or runner, about 20 inches by 46 inches, has a opportunistic design built around two half-rounds cut from a collar, and a matching edging used as a diagonal that connects them. Slight differences in the design of these laces say they were made as a set, probably a full round collar and matching flounce.

Connoisseur's Choice

This is very much a connoisseur's piece, with marvelous little details in the design and quality of the materials, and quirky little details in the workmanship. A true connoisseur would overlook the damage and wear to the lace yardage because of the overarching quality of the piece in general. The overall runner cannot be mended. Many of the key pieces are handmade Point de Gaze needle lace which is almost impossible to repair. Each piece in the patchwork is significant and cannot be replaced without destroying the character of the overall design.

The overall patchwork design probably was established by what appear to be cut halves of a round collar of Point de Gaze needle lace. The diagonal across the center is a matching piece of Point de Gaze, but

Details in the technique and workmanship, such as the way the flowers from the whitework embroidery are allowed to overlap the edging, make the patchwork endlessly fascinating. Why the insert was not trimmed from behind the flower filling for a cleaner effect is even more curious. Other areas were also treated this way (see next page). Perhaps the lacemaker avoided cutting the fine handmade lace so it might someday be again recycled?

Gallery

Large section of whitework with lovely drawnwork swags defines each side of the patchwork.

designed and made as a straight length. The whole is bordered with deep edgings of Point de Gaze along the short sides, English Bucks Point on the long sides, Both have very unusual designs and probably are mid-nineteenth century. Reticella, probably dating to the nineteenth century, is surrounded by Flemish bobbin lace that might well be seventeenth or even eighteenth century. A close look with a microscope to determine which fibers are linen and which cotton might help date the laces.

The technique and workmanship are uneven, begging the question "whatever

Gallery

were they thinking!" Some sections are meticulously worked, with seams that are turned and rolled on the back; other areas have wide, comparatively clumsy seams.

The only explanation I can come up with is that the lacemaker who was assembling the patchwork was reluctant to do any more cutting than necessary, on the chance that the fine handmade lace would one day again be recycled.

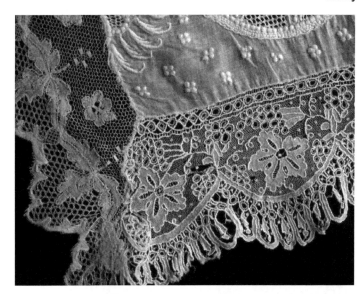

Above: Two different styles of lace, point de gaze and Bucks Point, meet in an unevenly mitered corner. There may, however, be a logic to how the point was constructed.

Right: A close look at the corner shows that the lacemaker respected the lines of the Point de Gaze lace (bottom of the corner and right) and avoided cutting through the relatively strong line of the clothwork when cutting the corner. A pretty point to the corner was achieved while still maintaining the visually and structurally strong lines of the handmade lace.

Note also the significant tears and breaks along the edge. Nearly all the lace has damage.

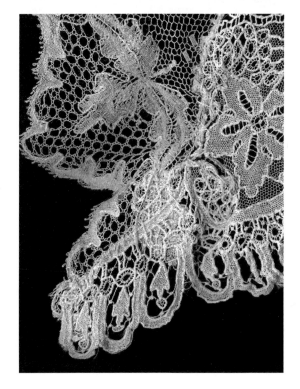

Gallery

Whatever were they thinking? Why would the lacemaker have run the curve of lace out into the border, then not cut away the lace behind it?

One possibility: to allow the fine handmade lace to be endlessly recycled. Even after it was used in this patchwork, it could easily be taken apart. The large whip or overcast stitches, made with relatively heavy, very visible thread easily could be undone, and the lace pieces salvaged yet one more time.

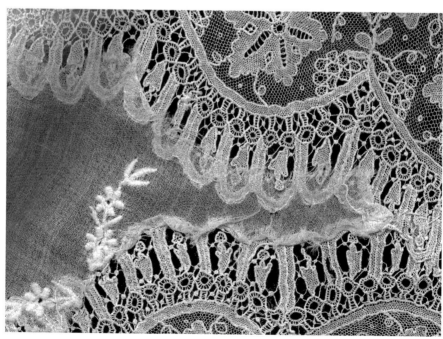

Gallery

Seams were simply whip stitched or overcast with heavy thread. In the section above, the sewing thread was not trimmed away. Cut edges in this area were either trimmed very close, or turned and overcast. This makes the lines between the laces very sharp and distinct when viewed from the front.

Opposite page: Not all cut edges were turned and overcast, or even trimmed close. In this area, the cut edges of the whitework where left at least a quarter to a half inch wide. These cut edges do show through and muddy the lines behind the open areas on the Point de Gaze it connects to. This inconsistency is unexplainable.

Mother's Prize

Photos courtesy of Devon M. Thein. Tablecloth is owned by Genevieve Kelly

A charming family history accompanies this tablecloth: the mother of the current owners won the tablecloth at a society bazaar in the New York-New Jersey area in 1918. Newly arrived in the U.S. from Poland, and working as a domestic, her employer took her to the event. The price listed on the tag reads $200, the equivalent of several months wages at the time. The lucky winner treasured her prize and often spoke of how highly the fair-goers respected the lace tablecloth. It is telling that she kept it instead of cashing in.

The diameter of the tablecloth is about 5 feet. It is made almost entirely of handmade laces, including Bruges and Valenciennes bobbin lace, Reticella and other needle laces, and filet lace. The technique and workmanship of each of the laces is very good, but not superb. All are good upper middle class laces. Several of the pieces are uncut, indicating that the design was worked around those key pieces.

All the materials in the tablecloth were typical of handmade laces being made in the early twentieth century. The old price tag also provides an interesting glimpse into its value at the time it was made; and begs to be compared to a value today. It would probably bring more in the market broken up into its pieces.

Gallery

Tablecloth center is formed of nice quality bobbin lace embellished with whitework inserts.

Endless surprises including a royal face worked in filet lace.

Gallery

Whitework inserts were carefully selected and fitted areound the bobbin lace flowers. Bobbin lace has flowers, leaves, and segmented scrolls typical of Bruges bobbin lace. Background of double braids in a hexagonal arrangement also is typical of Bruges. The very heavy outline or "gimp" thread is typical of a Belgian lace sometimes called Miracourt, a heavy, bold bobbin lace popular in the late nineteenth century. It is not especially rare to find late nineteenth century Belgian laces that are hybrids of more than one style.

Gallery

Side ovals were assembled around lace squares and other edgings, insertions, and cut lace pieces.

Detail of handmade needle lace fitted into the triangle of the side ovals. Motif is allowed to overlap the lace insertions that surround it.

After the War Was Over

This tablecloth came marching home from The Great War with their own family doughboy according to family lore. Although neither the style of the patchwork nor the materials are at all like those found in classic or commercial European patchworks, a date circa 1918 to 1920 would be very appropriate for all the materials in the tablecloth.

Without documentation, however, the stories told about the origins of the tablecloth are irrelevant. The quirky tablecloth generates plenty of stories on its own. The

Gallery

design is erratic and naive, the technique and workmanship quirky at best. The materials are nothing special and a bit the worse for wear. Nevertheless, peculiarities of the construction and materials give the tablecloth huge amounts of charm and mystery.

The joy of lace patchworks is not necessarily classic beauty, but the joy of discovery. Just when we might be prepared to dismiss this tablecloth as inferior, something raises our eyebrows and makes us take another closer look. The anomalies in technique and materials make it impossible to know what is original and what is a repair. Lace in the corners include mismatched styles and techniques.

Were the odd motifs in the design put there because there was not quite enough of some other lace to make ends meet, or does it signal a repair? Are the huge untrimmed lace pieces that overlap on the back the result of a careless repair, or did the original maker figure it hardly showed from the front and which buyer would really look that close?

Huge areas of the sides are composed of machine made lace, especially chemical lace that is beginning to deteriorate. Other large areas of lace don't really fit the design

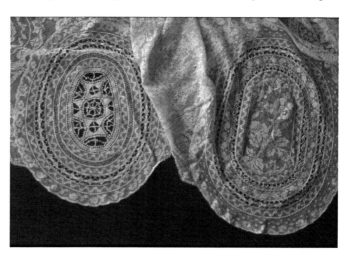

Lace pieces in corners are different.

Handmade filet lace is considered a homespun craft lace. Charming butterflies with wonderful long antennae that hide in the design add a surprise touch.

Gallery

overall. Did the original maker just use whatever they had at hand, or was someone repairing the piece at some later date that responsible for the strange features?

There are huge areas of background filled with machine made yardage, but not of the type used in commercially made lace patchworks. There is more variety, less homogeneity. It may not be particularly sophisticated, but is it interesting. For all its quirks and flaws, the tablecloth makes a great show on a large table.

Corners have odd side pieces that don't match. These might be repairs, or might fill in for a too-short background section. Note large untrimmed overlap.

Tape lace motif matches those used in other corresponding corners. Curious fill-in patch, however, does not match. Several areas have the deep overlap with untrimmed edges in the laces. This could mean many of these were original, and the workmanship was less than meticulous. Or it could mean lots of repairs.

Gallery

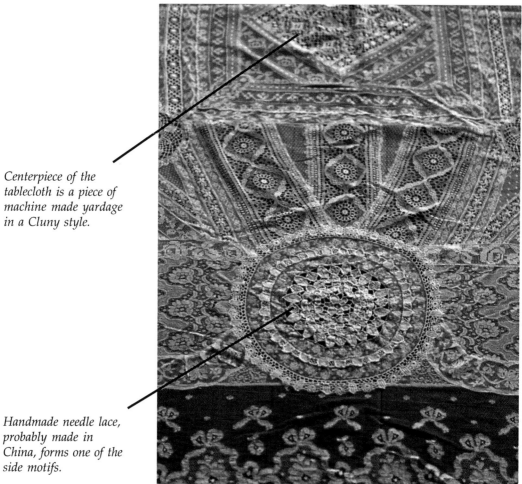

Centerpiece of the tablecloth is a piece of machine made yardage in a Cluny style.

Handmade needle lace, probably made in China, forms one of the side motifs.

Vive le Difference

Patchwork placemats: the same, only different. See page 45 for a full view of one of the placemats.

Studying sets of lace patchworks emphasizes a fundamental difference between calico fabric patchworks and lace patchworks. Matched or coordinated sets reveal interesting facets of the process of designing and making patchworks, and the effect of the pattern and texture of the material on the overall design.

Placemats on this opposite page, and doilies on the next page all have different arrangements of the same or similar laces. The laces at left include Duchesse bobbin lace, filet lace, and tape lace made from a segmented tape, along with Valenciennes lace edging.

Gallery

Such sets are rare. Few people have any use for sets, and collectors are content to have one of a kind. Dealers can get far more per piece when the sets are broken up so there is no incentive to even try to keep them together.

This particular set of placemats and doilies is remarkable for the overall good quality of the handmade laces used to make them, and the fascinating way the texture and pattern of each piece of lace is used to enhance the overall design of the patchwork.

The complexity of the design achieved in such a small space, and the unusual quality of the handmade laces makes each piece stand alone for quality. Put together, the entire set makes a dazzling show.

Each doily has the same handmade bobbin lace for an edging. Good quality mostly hamdmade laces compose each design. Each has some laces that match those in placemats on previous page. Tricks for designing intriguing patchworks are emphasized in the reversed images on the opposite page.

Gallery

Using the pattern of the lace as well as the arrangement of the pieces creates complex designs in these small doilies.

Single Duchsse bobbin lace flower covers the center seam between two side pieces of filet. Tape lace on the sides provides scallops of clothwork, as well as bright "eyes" of filling stitches.

Narrow strips of machine lace form a clean seam between the rough edges of filet lace in the center and the tape lace pieces on the sides. Zig-zag pattern in the torchon bobbin lace along the sides adds a strong contrast with machine lace curves.

Strips of handmade torchon bobbin lace and bebilla knotted lace alternate around the edge of the doily. Zigzag pattern point outward.

Strips running alongside the square bobbin lace center create the illusion of curves; zig-zag pattern in side torchon bobbin lace enhances that illusion.

Le Baseball Diamond

This patchwork has five different cap backs, each of very fine quality French *fond du bonet* with exquisite needle lace embellishments in the large flowers.

The marvelous embroideries are arranged like a common baseball diamond and embedded in a background of exquisite but identical crescents and wedges of commercial whitework embroidery and other laces. Little touches in the workmanship, however raise even this predictable arrangement a bit above the mundane. Note how the "base paths" of embroidered net that each have one rose that slightly overlaps the corner round, creating just a slight bit of movement to the design.

Gallery

Whitework round has highly decorative drawnwork filling in the large center flower. Smaller side flowers have decorative tiny needle lace centers.

Small whitework section, bottom left, is one of many identical embroidered flowers used as background. These likely were handmade, but commercially produced in large quantitites.

Gallery

Crescent shaped whitework pieces that form the outside edges of the tablecloth all have the same design, simple and open in comparison to the dense heavily embellished large rounds. This is a strong clue that they were commercially produced.

One side of each of the "base path" lines overlaps into the lace surrounding the cap back. This perhaps was intended to give the overall design some movement. Detail of side crescent is shown above.

Floral Fireworks

Classic French patchwork tablecloth with a half dozen different cap backs of superb **fond du bonet**. Patchwork probably dates to the late nineteenth or early twentieth century. Size is approximately four feet squre.

Extraordinary whitework embroidery used in an unusual way makes this tablecloth interesting for collectors and for makers looking for inspiration.

Although we will perhaps never know who made the piece and where, we know from the features that it was very professionally and artistically done.

Compare the overall design and quality of this tablecloth with the following pieces, which have equally fabulous *fond du bonet,* but used in a more conventional way.

Market value of this tablecloth should be high – anywhere over a thousand dollars would not be unreasonable – because the quality of the materials is so extraordinary, and the design is unusually creative as well. The tablecloth would appeal both to users and to collectors.

Scallops that surround the center and shape the overall patchwork are unusual.

Little oddities punctuate the design and technique. Motifs (circled) occasionally are allowed to overlap the lace edging that shape the design.

Lots of patching was done to fill the spaces in the center, and in each side area.

Gallery

The whitework cap backs are spectacular, and each has a different pattern. Very dense patterns are embellished with a wide variety of needle lace fillings. Almost all of the surrounding laces are handmade, including a variety of handmade Valenciennes and Mechlin bobbin laces used to surround sections, and for the final border.

Gallery

Cutting out the background fabric and extending the flowers beyond their natural fabric border makes them look like luxurious bouquets exploding out of their holders.

Ouiseaux Extraordinaire

The bird is extraordinary; the peony it has chosen to alight on is amazing. The density of the embroidery gives it remarkable texture; the variety and complexity of the needle lace fillings are a delight.

Gallery

Overview of the extraordinary bird patchwork. Size of the piece is 21 inches by 25 inches.

Fabulous materials often are the highlight of classic French lace patchworks; the overall design of the patchwork may be trite. In this centerpiece, the bird alighting on a peony is *fond du bonet* as good as it gets.

It may well have been the intent of the maker to keep the overall patchwork design simple, to serve as a frame for the remarkable center.

The lopsided workmanship of the patchwork, however, is a surprising contrast to the exquisite work of the embroidery.

This provides an interesting insight into the times when this patchwork was made. Who today would dare recycle such a marvelous piece of embroidery.

Gallery

The amazing complexity and extremely fine stitching of vintage French whitework makes it very difficult to detect flaws and mends. The combination of very fine fabric, and dense, heavy embroidery meant the fabric almost always tore.

Tiny areas of darning are barely perceptible around the spectacular feathered bird.

Gallery

Each of the side panels is a different pattern of fond du bonet. *Such variety of fine quality whitework in a single small item like this centerpiece makes it quite rare, and a good collector's piece.*

Faux French

Spectacular whitework round is machine embroidered. Note embroidery that finishes the round edge; this does not appear on fond du bonet *rounds rescued from old cap backs.*

Fabulous fakery, a machine imitation of a *fond du bonet* round cap back, is the attraction of this patchwork. "Real" *fond du bonet*, French cap backs from Normandy and Brittany with their heavy embroidery and fanciful inserts of needle lace are the stars of classic French patchworks.

Machine-embroidered imitations of *fond du bonet* are not found in vintage caps. It is a remarkable testimony to the popularity of Normandy Lace patchworks that an industry would have been developed to imitate those cap backs by machine.

This level of machine embroidery was a time consuming and complex process. In its day, it would have been expensive to produce and would be nearly impossible to duplicate today.

Long trailing strips of lace along one side suggest the large rectangle was salvaged from a larger piece, perhaps a bedspread. It

Above: Overview of rectangular fragment. Trailing remnants of long edging along one side suggest it was salvaged from a larger piece, most likely a bedspread.

Gallery

is large enough to make a decent pillow sham, but the poor, shredded condition of the center round makes this remnant difficult to use. The embroidered round would need to be supported with a silk gauze for it to survive a wash and possible use.

The main interest of this piece is as a curiosity: a fabulous fake! The value of the overall piece is minimal because of the condition. Even in tattered and torn condition, however, the center round is well worth saving for the story it has to tell.

A back closeup view of the center embroidery shows uneven lines down the embroidered petals where the bobbin thread caught the top thread – clear evidence of machine embroidery.

The lace filling in the flower center has the slightly fuzzy appearance of the machine blatt stitch, rather than the distinct buttonhole stitches that would appear in a hand stitched needle lace filling.

Edging and insertion laces in very similar patterns, both fairly convincing machine imitations of bobbin lace, suggest this was a commercial patchwork.

Gallery

Whitework is darned with a very thick thread, possibly an embroidery floss.

Two different patterns of Irish Crochet were used in the patchwork, as well as filet lace. Center strip is a very delicately machine embroidered insertion.

Grace

The exact age of this graceful little cape is not known, but certainly these were in style in the late nineteenth , and up to the beginning of the twentieth centuries.

So many styles of pieced work were made, trying to decide what to call Normandy Lace is pointless.

The shape is a square with rounded corners formed around a small round collar. Deep flounce pieces were joined with wide lace insertions which radiate from the small Bedfordshire lace collar.

The fragile condition and many tears and breaks in the lace and whitework keep it from being a great wearable cape, and would keep the market value down, but the graceful shape, supple materials, and overall beautiful design offer inspiration for ways to copy it in newer materials.

Motifs were cut from antique bobbin lace, probably eighteenth century, stitched to the embroidered muslin fabric, and the back of the flowers was cut away. The placement is relatively random. Whether they were intended to cover holes in the deep whitework flounce that forms the cape, or simply added as decoration, will never be known.

Grecian Ladies

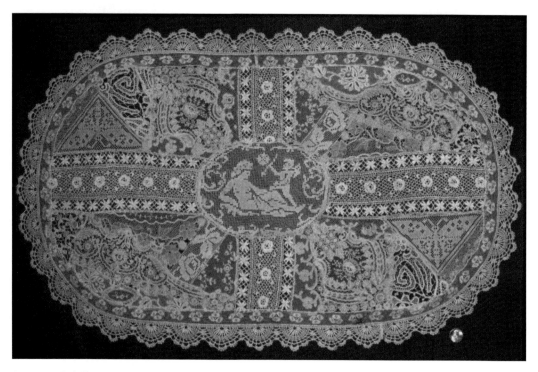

Large oval doily or centerpiece, about 22 inches by 18 inches.

The center motif, the bold and somewhat unusual arrangement of the laces, plus the choice of nice middle-class handmade laces raises the question, could this possibly be a Greek lace mosaic?

For this author Greek lace mosaics remain a curiosity seen only in books (*Lace in Chios*, by Despina Koutsakis) Nevertheless, this piece does have those similarities.

A combination of handmade and machine made laces, including Mixed Brussels bobbin and needle lace, Irish crochet, and edged with handmade Cluny bobbin lace in a classic scallop pattern.

The usefullness of this piece – it would display splendidly – along with the wonderful assortment of handmade laces increase the value. The possiblity that it might be a Greek lace mosaic also adds to the intrigue.

Gallery

A semi-crazy patchwork fills each quarter of the design. Opposite corners are approximately symmetrical. Filet lace butterfly adds an amusing detail. Center area has a large piece of Brussels Mixed lace, a combination of Duchesse bobbin lace with Point de Gaze needle lace insert; essentially a piecework within a patchwork. Cross pieces are Cluny bobbin lace and Irish crochet.

Living With Lace Patchworks

The whole point of "sharing, using, blending" vintage lace pieces is to have them out, visible, enjoyed, and seen.

Each object should be carefully inspected, judged for quality, and evaluated for condition. Whether something can be used as originally intended or should be carefully preserved depends on the characteristics of that individual piece. Commercially produced patchworks from the 1920s and 1930s usually can be happily used. Classic French with fine whitework usually is too valuable and fragile for use.

Small pillow shams, boudoir pillows, runners, and doilies most often should be seen, displayed, and used. In all cases, remember the age of these pieces, and treat them gently.

Lace patchwork bedspreads might be reserved for use in a guest room where they may be seen but less often handled. A bedspread might be mounted on a sheer color fabric to reduce stress of lifting, shifting, and folding when the bed is used and the linens changed.

Boudoir pillows typically are overstuffed into rigid mounds. To prevent tearing the seams unstuff the pillow or put a slip or liner over the pillow to absorb the stress. Slip the lace loosely over the liner.

Washing and mending can be good for many lace patchworks. Gentle, careful use is usually better than the most benign neglect.

Photo left: Section of a boudoir pillow with commercial fond du bonet *and other very fine embroidery and machine lace. The repair of this piece is featured in this section.*

Professional help is available for those with no time or no suitable facilities for washing, drying, or mending. For washing and cleaning estimates contact:

Linens Limited
240 N. MilwaukeeSt.
Suite 401
Milwaukee, WI 53202
414-223-1123
www.thelaundryat.com

Gentle Arts - Uptown
4500 Dryades St.
New Orleans, LA 70115
504-895-5628
www.gentleartsneworleans.com

For mending consultation and estimates, contact:

The Lace Merchant
ekurella@elizabethkurella.com
www.lacemerchant.com

Washing

Washing a patchwork of old laces poses a few special problems. Some laces hundreds of years old may be mixed in with newer pieces. Nevertheless, patchworks of lace often have to be washed to make them clean enough to use, enjoy, and live with. Often they must be washed before mending in order to see what color the laces really are, and to select a patch of the right shade of white to blend with the remaining patchwork. Washing also will tell if stains will come out. If they do not, the choice may be to live with the stains, or to replace the stained piece. Bleaching a whole item to treat small localized stains is a bad choice. The bleach will weaken the overall patchwork, and may not even remove the stain. A good choice usually is to live with a few flaws, rather than stress the entire patchwork.

■ **Inspect and evaluate the whole piece.** Consider this a chance to stop and inspect the roses, admire the designs, marvel at the handwork. At the same time, note and mark any trouble spots, especially pieces that are especially weak, or backed with net or some other support fabric.

■ **Plan the washing.** Think about what is involved in the washing process, what might happen to the patchwork, and what will be done with the wet, washed bundle.

The weight of the water can tear fragile laces. The fragile wet mass will need a suitable place to drain, then a suitable space to be spread for drying.

■ **Support and stabilize.** The patchwork may need to be stabilized with some stitching before washing, and certainly supported in the wash. The final mending usually must be done after washing, so the actual color can be determined and mending threads matched.

Small pieces might be basted loosely onto a large piece of tulle or net. Place tablecloths and bedspreads in a wash tub already lined with a clean old sheet or other fabric. When it comes time to lift the patchwork out of the wash water, lift the liner. This supports the more fragile patchwork.

If possible, drain the water out of the tub first, then left out the wet bundle.

■ **Wash.** If the material is particularly dirty, plan to soak it for hours, perhaps days, several times. Detergents and cleaning agents can come later, after the worst of the dirt is soaked out.

A unique balancing act must play out. Some chemical action – acid or base – must force apart the twisted fibers and coax out the stain or dirt particles. This acid or base also is going to weaken the fibers. The trick is to use as little chemical action as possible while getting out the dirt.

The same goes for agitation. With more agitation more dirt may be coaxed out, but chance of damage to the fiber increases. Minimize agitation by swirling or gently hand squeezing.

Many fibers were not white white to begin with. Over the years, they naturally oxidize and darken.

Early instructions called for a tea and coffee dye to get the shades of white and ecru to match. Others used powdered ochre to gave a pale rust tone to the overall lace. These dyes will not come out, no matter how the lace is washed or bleached.

■ **Choose a washing product.** Every grandmother's home remedy from buttermilk to sea water, lemon juice, salt, grass, boiling and cold water washes has been studied and the active ingredients turned into commercial products. The advantage of using a commercial product rather than a home-brew is that the commercial product generally will be more predictable and uniform. The disadvantage is the unknown extras: perfumes, colorings, and artificial whiteners.

Enzymes and bleaches like Oxyclean and Biz were designed for new fibers, and may be are too harsh for vintage lace. Most also have artificial optical whiteners which add chemicals to the fiber to fool the eye into seeing bright white. These give the vintage lace an artificial bright white appearance that forever after marks the fabric as bleached.

Choose the gentlest agent that will do the job. Orvus is a neutral pH shampoo that will do no harm. However, it rarely gets things as clean as we would like.

Whichever product is used, rinse, rinse, and rinse again.

■ **Dry.** Place the wet bundle somewhere most of the water can drain away before trying to open out the lace.

After the lace has drained for an hour or even longer, until it is simply damp rather than soaking wet, carefully open it out and spread it out to dry. Hand press or block it into shape on large towels, perhaps covered with a clean sheet.

■ **Iron.** Press patchworks only from the back side, with the lace and embroidery face-down on a fluffy towel so it will not be flattened.

Be very careful not to snag the point of the iron on seams, and connecting bars in the piecework. A pressing cloth helps prevent snagging, and keeps dirt and starch from the iron off the lace.

For large, awkward pieces, recruit a friend to help. They can help by holding up parts of those pieces, keeping them from tangling in the cord, and away from possible snags.

Mending

Simple large overcast or whip stitches are all that hold most lace patchworks together. Edges on the back typically were cut close and left raw. Expect split seams and shredding edges as well as whatever besets old laces.

The very seams that can easily split make the patchworks possible to repair. Simple unraveling seams are easily restitched. Badly stained, torn, dry rotted or shredding pieces of lace often can be removed and replaced.

Decades ago, the classic technique for mending Normandy patchworks was to stitch tulle to the back side to support the damaged area. This stabilized the piece,

and made it possible to continue to use the item. One big disadvantage: the tulle has texture and pattern of its own. The tulle's grid-like pattern shows through, creates a visual static, and interferes with designs in the lace and sheer embroideries.

Repairing or replacing the damaged areas often are a better alternative, and not that difficult to do. Consider the possibility of repairing even those pieces already marked with patches of tulle by replacing the deteriorated sections.

First consider whether or not the item should be repaired, then consider the possibilities for mending.

To mend or not to mend

After the condition of the patchwork has been evaluated, and the damage assessed, a little thought should go into deciding whether or not the patchwork can, or should be mended.

■ **What kind of patchwork is it?** Museum-quality pieces usually should be left as is, or repaired by professionals.
Some jobs end up bigger than expected. Commercial patchworks usually are symmetrical, and significant damage to

any element may mean replacing all the matching pieces in other parts of the piecework. Artisanal or crazy-patchworks usually can be altered with less difficulty.

■ **Why are you thinking of fixing it?** To continue to use it in its original form may require a different mend than those intended for passive display. Pieces that will be viewed closely might get a different, more precise repair than those that will only be viewed from a distance.

The repair problems described in this book are those most typical of lace patchworks. For more information about mending lace, see the author's book, *Anybody Can Mend Lace and Linens*, available at www.lacemerchant.com

Living with Lace Patchworks

Keys to Any Successful Mend
In addition to basic sewing techniques, there is a process to follow to assure a successful mending job.

■ **Fill the Spaces.** Separated pieces should not be drawn together to fill a space. This distorts the design, creating stress that will cause more damage.

Find a way that fills in any missing material while keeping the lines of the design in mind.

■ **Maintain the Lines.** Lines in patchworks are defined by insertions of lace edgings outlining sections and focus pieces. The lines of threads defining patterns in the lace also contribute to the overall patchwork design. If any of these lines are distorted, the design suffers.

■ **Match the color and texture.** Any mend that does not blend as closely as possible with the original color, weight of the thread, and texture of the lace will stand out. Duplicating the original stitches is the least important concern.

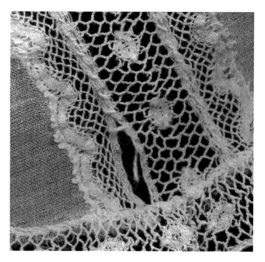

Separations in joins between two lace insertions with finished edges are the most common problem with lace patchworks. They also are easiest to mend. Simply sew the two edges together again with overcast or whip stitches, just as they originally were stitched. A common sewing thread was most often used.

Work Surface for Mending
When mending small areas of lace, a good work surface that will not catch the needle is a folded piece of dark fabric with a small patch of clear adhesive plastic. The work can be basted or pinned to the fabric for stitching, and the needle will not catch on the plastic. The dark color makes it easier to see the work.

Living with Lace Patchworks

Repair or replace
a damaged section?

This wacky, quasi-crazy patchwork was badly made to begin with, it was terribly damaged and already had so many replaced pieces it was impossible to know what it originally looked like.

The scattering of secret little butterflies as well as the potential of the center section made it irresistable to mend.

Making it presentable enough to display as a wall hanging involved both repairing and replacing pieces.

Above and right: Little butterflies are hiding everywhere is this patchwork. Some are filet lace insertions, other are simply shaped pieces of lace.

Living with Lace Patchworks

Consider replacing pieces when:

■ Pieces are dry-rotted or worn out and too weak to support a repair.

■ Suitable replacement pieces are available.

■ The damaged pieces do not define the design or character of the patchwork and another kind of lace can be substituted.

■ Pieces are not so large or interconnected with other pieces that the structure of the whole would be disrupted.

Consider repairing the damage when:

■ Damage is not severe, and is easy to repair.

■ The existing lace is strong, and will support repairs.

■ The patterns in the original lace are important to the overall design, and cannot be duplicated.

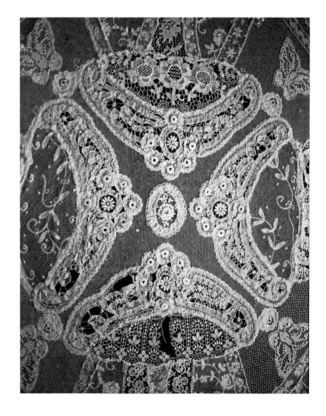

The four tape lace insertions that define the center all have damage. Tape lace, however, is generally easy to repair. (See Anybody Can Mend Lace and Linens *by the author for specific techniques for mending tape lace.)*

The two chemical lace pieces at the top and bottom are dry rotted and shredding — not to mention they do nothing for the design. Applique lace like that in the two side pieces is relatively easy to find, and would make a good replacement for the top and bottom pieces.

Living with Lace Patchworks

Replacing a Patchwork Section
Replacing damaged pieces often is not difficult. Lace patchworks most often were put together with long overcast stitches. In reality, this means they are just basted together. Repairing is a simple matter of out with the old, in with the new!

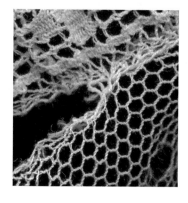

Out with the old:
Just clip the original stitches, and remove the old piece.

A few more tips:

■ **Maintain the original space.** It can be helpful to make a photocopy of the section before the old piece is removed, to provide a pattern, especially for large or odd shaped areas. Pin or baste the patchwork to shape on a paper or other work surface before inserting the new piece.

■ **Cutting the new piece:** Trace the hole in the patchwork to make a pattern, or make a photocopy of the original patchwork, and cut the area out to use as a pattern.

■ **Choosing the replacement part.** Make a photocopy of available lace, and try it out as a replacement. Cut the copy to fit the space to see if there is enough lace for the job, to see if the texture and pattern blend.

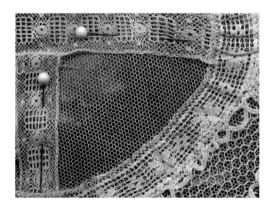

In with the new:
Cut the new piece about a quarter inch bigger than the space on each side. Slip the piece into the space, and pin it in place.

Stitch the new piece in place with fairly long overcast or whip stitches. Trim the edges to a neat quarter inch on the back.

Repairing frayed, split seams in lace

A cut edge separated from the adjacent lace insertion often frays just a bit, and the lace thus becomes just slightly smaller than the space it fills. Drawing these pieces together again will cause tension and more fraying.

Reinforce the frayed edge with a couple of rows of running stitches made with a very fine thread to stabilize the edge, and darn over the edge as the seam is repaired.

A slightly frayed edge along a separated seam is a typical problem.

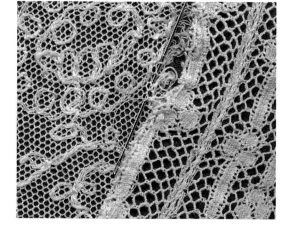

Reinforce the edge of the net with rows of running stitches, using very fine thread that will not be visible..

Living with Lace Patchworks

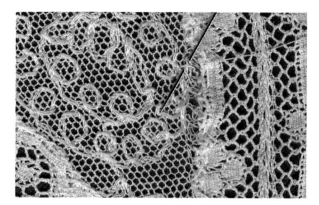

Mend the gap by darning over the reinforced edge.

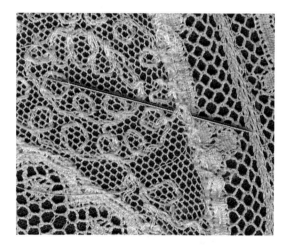

The reinforced and darned lace insert should be just brought up to the edge of the adjacent lace without stress or pulling. Whip stitch both edges together.

Living with Lace Patchworks

Repairing frayed, split seams in whitework

The split seams very often are in the whitework pieces that define the design of the overall patchwork. The fine muslin fabric becomes frayed along the edge, and it often cannot be darned.

One fairly easy solution is to remove the whitework piece, add very narrow insertion of lace or net to make the opening smaller, and replace the section. The choice of filler will depend on the overall design of the patchwork, and the size and design of the fabric round.

Do not trim away frayed edges of the round. Any little bit of fabric or threads may be helpful in replacing it. They can be trimmed after it is stitched back in place.

Whitework rounds were whip stitched into place in vintage patchworks, and the edges trimmed close on the back. The sheer fragile edges typically fray. Removing the round, making the hole smaller, and replacing the original piece often is easier and cheaper than finding and buying a replacement.

Living with Lace Patchworks

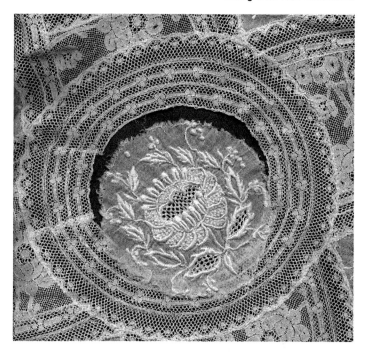

To make the hole smaller before reinserting the whitework round a tiny, simple insert was called for.

To avoid drawing attention from the whitework, a simple narrow insertion of plain net was used to make the center hole slightly smaller.

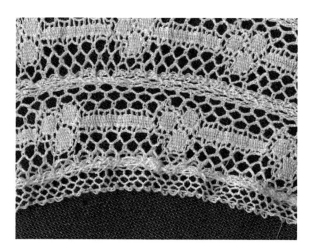

Living with Lace Patchworks

Whitework round was pinned in position before stitching in place.

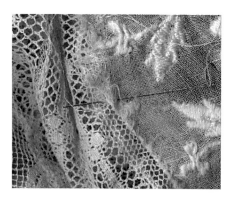

The raw edge on the back was turned and overcast to keep it from unraveling and shredding. It was not done in vintage pieces. It is helpful, however, to keep the fine muslin from shredding.

Carefully secure the patchwork and repositioned piece on a working surface, such as a dark fabric covered with a piece of plastic, to keep it properly oriented while the section is stitched in place.

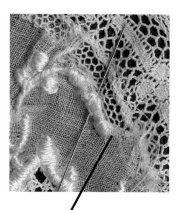

The raw edge was initially left in the front and tucked under the edge as it was stitched in place. Working from the front made it easier to keep the piece positioned.

The tendrils and leaflets that extend out were allowed to overlap the edge when the section is replaced. The practical reason: this very heavy bit of embroidery hits right at the seam line, and is hard to cut and stitch. Artistically, the whitework already has become rather small when the edge was trimmed and the tiny insertion place around it. Allowing the tendril to break out into the outline continues the flow of the design.

Living with Lace Patchworks

Repairing Damaged Whitework

Almost all vintage whitework has holes and tears. The fine translucent fabric used as the base for the *fond du bonet* whitework embroidery often was too delicate to support the embroidery.

Vintage pieces very often are found darned and patched. Similar darning and patching, when done carefully and thoughtfully, often is a better choice than backing the entire piece of whitework with tulle or fabric, which slightly obscures the overall design.

Keys to successfully darning and mending are the basic guidelines for any repair: fill the space, maintain the lines, and match the color and texture.

Tiny patch of very fine fabric was inserted behind the frayed hole above the coin. Patch could be further hidden by embroidering a satin stitch leaf at the end of the tendril. Back view of patch is shown at right.

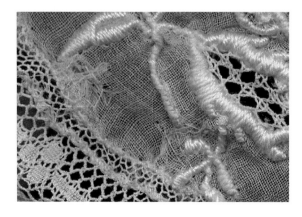

Only a few threads run through the fabric will be enough to stabilize the tear and create a suitable edge for pieces to be displayed. It will not be strong enough for pieces that will continue to be used.

141

Living with Lace Patchworks

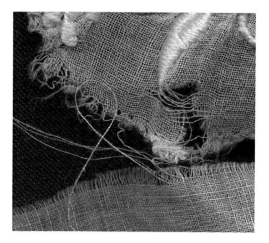

Needles and thread
for mending whitework

The right choice of needles and threads makes all the difference between a successful, unobtrusive mend and an obvious one.

A thread that is much too thick and heavy will make an obvious mend. Using a thread much finer and thinner than that used to make the lace in the first place is the best choice. This makes it possible to take many stitches, and "sneak up" on a mend with the work not showing.

Drawing a few warp threads out of a scrap of old fabric as fine or finer than the fabric being mended may be the best source of the thread fine enough for mending.

Bead needles often are the finest that can readily be found, and they are good for darning fine whitework. Heavier needles will punch holes and further damage the fabric.

Repair or patch a torn mesh-based lace?

Lace insertions and edgings with a mesh background are a major element in vintage lace patchworks.

Tears and holes in the mesh are a very typical problem. Check for dry rot. If the lace tears easily, it will need to be replaced.

If a good, sound lace just was accidentally torn, or has a hole punched in it, it often can be fixed. There are two choices: put in a patch, or repair the hole.

Very small tears or holes, a half inch or less in length, generally are best repaired. Large holes may be better patched.

■ Repairing a Torn Lace With a Mesh Background

There typically are two parts to any lace mend: rebuilding the clothwork, or dense area of the pattern, and repairing the background mesh.

Always keep the key rules in mind: fill the space, maintain the lines, and match the color and texture.

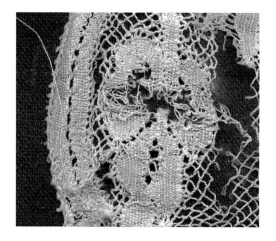

Living with Lace Patchworks

■ **To mend a very small tear in the mesh**
Choose a thread much finer than the thickness of the mesh. Working diagonally, along the lines of the mesh, darn across the break. Do not pull the pieces together.

■ **To mend clothwork areas**
Shredded threads were stitched in place with a kind of pseudo-darning using very fine thread. Darning stitches were run in the same direction as the original weaving.

Pressing the lace will flatten tufts in the darning.

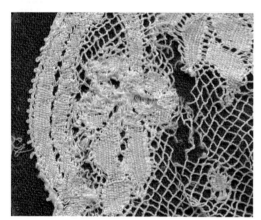

Any rebuilt little bits of mesh were aligned in the same direction as those in the original mesh.

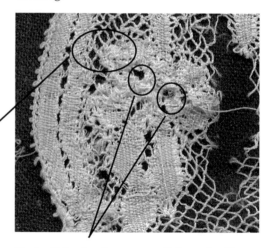

Parts of the darning were pulled apart with overcast stitches to mimic the pattern of little holes in the original leaf.

Living with Lace Patchworks

■ **To mend a small hole in the mesh**
Choose the mesh for the patch. It must be an exact match to the original net. Be sure to match the shape of the mesh – square, rectangle, hexagon, or other; size of the mesh; weight of the threads.

Before cutting the patch, make sure it will be big enough to overap the hole by at least 4-5 mesh on all sides after it is aligned.

Put the lace with the hole over the patch. Align both meshes exactly, pin both pieces to the work surface to hold them in place, then baste both pieces to the work surface.

Use as fine a thread as possible to sew the patch and lace together. It must be significantly finer and lighter in weight than the meshes.

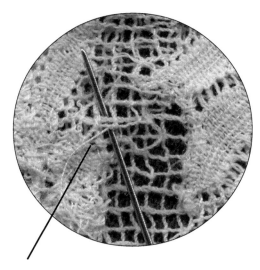

Working in and out of the overlapping meshes, attach the patch to the lace by whip stitching (overcasting) around each mesh, and along the edges of any cloth part of the lace.

Whip stitch over at least two rows of the mesh to be sure the patch is secure.

Carefully trim away close to the seam on both sides of the lace.

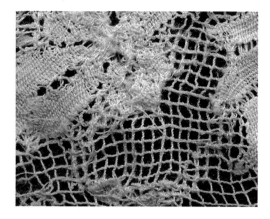

The imperfections of the completed patch job are visible on a very close look, but disappear nicely in a ruffled pillow edge.

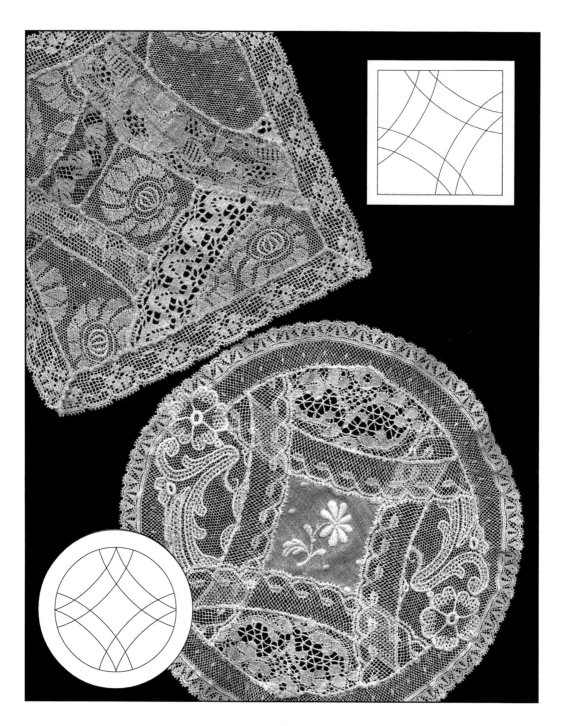

Making Lace Patchworks Today

Making a patchwork of lace is very different from making a fabric patchwork. Using a simple template for the first project will allow you to discover those differences quickly, and have fun exploiting them in one-of-a kind designs.

Each step in this process has a basic logic behind it, and each offers a whole raft of creative options and choices. Get a grip on the overall simple process, then study the possibilities each step offers.

Each piece of white lace not only has its own pattern, but it has color variations, shades and texture. The choice of lace bits to use in the patchwork will change the overall design even when you start with the same template. How the outline is basted to the template and how the spaces are filled in also can change the overall design.

Years of making dozens and dozens of lace patchworks have taught me that hand and machine sewing each have can have a place in making lace patchworks. Hand stitching the old-fashioned way works best for joining the lace pieces. Machine sewing can be a faster way to lay down the outline of the template and get on to the fun part putting the patchwork together.

Try the simple, quick overcast or whip stitch that traditionally was used to make lace patchworks. It is remarkably easy and fast. There is a simple logic to sewing that way and it provides certain benefits specific to lace patchworks.

First of all, it can be taken apart very quickly. Make a mistake, and you can undo it. Change your mind about the design, and you can change it. I discovered this when I was trying to repair an old, worn out lace patchwork and realized how easily damaged, stained, or worn out pieces could be replaced. Replacing them changed the design, and suddenly I was making new patchworks.

The simple hand stitching also disappears nicely into the complexities of the lace design. Any time I have tried stitching by machine the effect was not as clean, nor as soft and supple as hand stitching. It left a more defined outline around the edge of each piece. Plus, in the long run, with all the stabilizing required, machine stitching the lace pieces together was not much faster than the simple overcast stitch .

Thus the instructions I offer are for hand stitching. Learn the basic process, enjoy the creative options, then experiment with methods of your own. This is a folk art. There are no absolute rights and wrongs, only play. Above all, there are no lace police!

Opposite page: The same basic template can be worked in many different ways, and is an easy, fast way to start making lace patchworks.

Preparing the Lace

Using scraps of too-good-to throw away old lace in patchworks is very satisfying and rewarding. It is a joy to see them get a new life, and the variety of types and designs is thrilling. Plus, the price often is right.

Decide on the look you want as you consider washing the lace. Bleaching may unify the color and produce a brighter white. It will however weaken the lace. There also is no turning back from bleaching. Once the graceful old off-whites have been bleached the lace no longer looks antique. No amount of follow-up tea dying will replace that.

■ **Washing yardage.** Stashes of dirty old lace still are available for reasonable prices – but they do require an investment of time and effort to wash.

Carefully fold long lengths of yardage, and stitch or pin them into loose skeins. Loose yardage will form spaghetti-like masses in the wash. Soak old lace in tubs or bowls of warm water.

Skeins of wet yardage can be blocked or pulled into shape and wound around glasses or bottles to dry. Even the most carefully blocked yardage, however, most likely will need to be ironed to be flat and straight enough to use.

■ **Be creative with color.** White has a remarkable range of shades and tones. Be flexible about blending shades of white and ecru into patchworks. The most beautiful and interesting patchworks include many different shades. This emphasizes and enhances differences in texture and pattern. Experiment with a making a couple of patchworks in shades of white before trying any drastic bleaching or coloring of the lace.

In the early years of the twentieth century, it was fashionable to unify the color by tea dying or coloring with iron oxide. These were all permanent coloring techniques, and ultimately damage the fibers. The brown and dark ecru shades so popular at the time are now completely out of fashion, and great damage is done to the patchwork in trying to bleach them out.

Preparing to Play!

We stretch out and limber up before embarking on a run or exercise session. Here are a couple of exercises to help turn loose the creativity.

A good patchwork design has a focus, some background, and something to hold it all together.

Spread your stash out on a table or the floor like a deck of cards and play with the pieces. If there is a sentimental favorite heirloom piece that simply must go in the patchwork, start with that and play around it.

Sort out pieces with shades of white that blend well together. Try for natural blending before thinking of bleaching or dying. Natural almost always gives a more pleasant result!

What kind of yardage is available to create the outline? Is enough available? Which pieces have the strongest design, and would make good focus pieces? Finding lace to serve quietly as the background and not steal attention from the focus usually is the hardest detail to solve.

In a good patchwork design, there is enough contrast so the lines and spaces show up well. Separate dense and open pieces. Sort pieces by texture, density and visual weight.

Consider the lines of the template pattern. Are there pieces of lace with patterns that complement those lines, or could serve as accents to highlight the lines? Shuffle the deck and start over. See what wants to go together.

Finally, spend plenty of time playing with the laces in different light. Subtle stains may only show up in sunlight or with the right side light. Colors, especially shades of white, look different in different lights. Play in the daytime and again at night to see the effect.

The time spent playing with the lace will be well rewarded with many good design possibilities. Don't be surprised if more than one patchwork wants to be made!

Step by Step

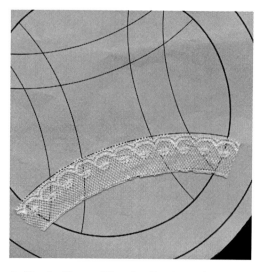

1. Baste the outline to the template.

2. Fill the spaces with lace or sheer embroidered fabric.

3. Stitch the pieces together.

Making Lace Patchworks Today

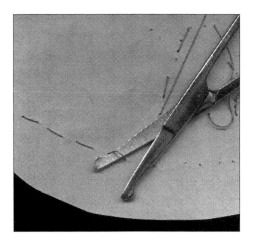

4. Cut the basting stitches and...

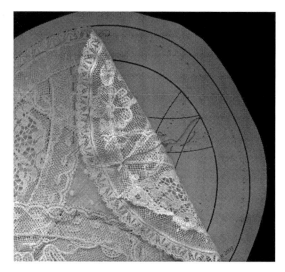

...remove the patchwork.

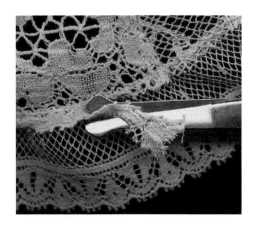

5. Trim the edges to about a quarter inch of the seam.

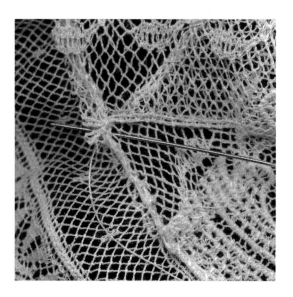

6. Roll and overcast the edges to more sharply define the lines.

Making Lace Patchworks Today

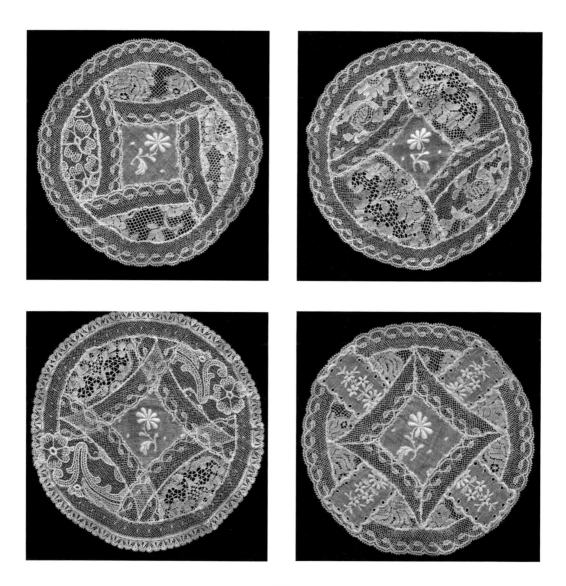

Making Lace Patchworks Today

Opposite page: Four different ways of working the same template of four overlapping curves.

INDEX OF ILLUSTRATIONS

This is a book of show-and-tell. The index tells you where to find the pictures that tell stories and explain concepts.

American Artisanal........................15-18, 24
    Bows and Buttons............................66-68
    Emily's Missing Masterpieces.........76-77
    Mary Martin's Mother's Tablecloth...64-65
    Rose Anne's Round...........................69-71
    Simple Gifts....................................56, 58-59
    Texas Treasures................................62-63
    Unfinished Symphony.....................60-61

Artists
    Artkamper, Mrs.................................20-21
    Bohassek, Mrs. K..............................20-21
    Cavander, Blanche Phillipe............62-63
    Colonial Coverlet Guild...................20-21
    Hadley, Sara...16,18
    Moraitakis, Mrs...22
    Mary Martin's Mother...........................64
    Millard, Molly....................................17-18
    Stefanou, Mrs. K.......................................22
    Teagle, Emily...76
    Whitcomb, Edna Wilson.............….20

Chios, Island of, Greek Lace Mosaics....22-23

Classic French...10
    Author's patchwork...........................11, 40
    Le Baseball Diamond..................107-109
    Floral Fireworks...........................110-113
    Oiseaux Extraordinaire...............117-117

Commemorative 20-21

Commercial European.............................12-13
    Opportunistic..21
      After the War Was Over.................100-103
      Collector's Quarry............................86-89
      Connoisseur's Choice.......................90-95
      Mother's Prize...................................96-99
      Vive le Difference..........................104-106
    Template-based...........................13, 28-29
      Jane's Gift..78-79
      Le Baseball Diamond.................107-109
      Quartet...84-85
      Whitework Wonderland..................81-83

Condition................................51-52, 58, 60-61,
    67, 70, 93, 102, 116, 121, 123
    (see also mending)

Design 45-47
    (see also template-based and opportunistic)
    good design.......................................45-46
    bad design...45-48

European commercial, see Commercial

fond du bonet
    vintage French.............10-11, 33-35, 40,
      42, 72, 107-117

commercial whitework.............12, 36-37
machine made................................118-121

Greek Lace Mosaics..................................22-23
Grecian Lady...................................124,125

Judging..45-49, 51-52
(see design, materials, technique, workman-
ship, and condition)

Making, see technique

Materials
Background materials............................38
Commercial Whitework.................12, 33,
36-37,110-113,114-117
Focus..32
fond du bonet................10-11, 34-35, 110-117
Framework..12, 39
Machine lace background....................32
Machine lace insertions........................39

Mending
How-to
Frayed edges................................138
Replace pieces......................134-135
split seams....................131, 138-139
patch holes in whitework..........141
patch holes in lace..............143, 144

Recognizing in old patchworks..........51,
58, 102, 73, 75, 116, 121, 123

Opportunistic patchworks.............21, 30-31
see also Commercial European

Repairs, see mending

Structure of patchworks; see opportunistic
and template-based

Technique
in making today...............................150-154
in vintage patchworks........15, 18, 48-49,
58-59, 60, 68, 70, 85, 93-95, 109, 113, 123

Template-based patchworks.......28,-29, 76-77
see also Commercial European

Workmanship...48-49
see also Technique

Connoisseur's Guides to Vintage Lace
by Elizabeth M. Kurella

This new series is designed to break the secret codes that shroud lace in mystery.
Anyone willing to take a close look and consider the fine details can become a judge and scholar – a connoisseur – of lace.

All *Connoisseur's Guides* are 7 by 8 1/2 inches and have more than 100 black and white photos and illustrations.

Connoisseur's Guide to Whitework Embroidered Lace Handkerchiefs
ISBN 0-9642871-5-3

Connoisseur's Guide to Honiton Lace
ISBN 0-9642871-4-5

More books by *Elizabeth M. Kurella:*

 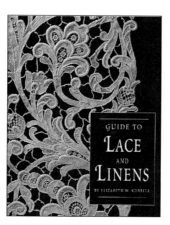 

Basic mending techniques presented step-by-step in detailed photos.

128 pages 8.5 by 11; more than 300 black and white photos; indexed.

A comprehensive guide to lace identification.

224 pages; 8.5 x 11 soft cover; 450 black and white photos; indexed

It's Back! The original guide that shows-and-tells the difference between handmade and machine.

76 pages; 8/5 x 11 soft cover; More than a hundred large black and white photos; indexed.

Order books from:
The Lace Merchant, Box 244, Whiting, IN 46394 or online at
www.lacemerchant.com